MASHIES AND MASH TUNS

MASHIES AND MASH TUNS

A WHISKY AND GOLF TOUR OF ENGLAND, WALES & IRELAND

ANDREW BROWN

YOUCAXTON PUBLICATIONS
OXFORD & SHREWSBURY

Copyright © Andrew Brown 2019

The Author asserts the moral right to
be identified as the author of this work.

ISBN 978-1-912419-75-3
Printed and bound in Great Britain.
Published by YouCaxton Publications 2019

All rights reserved. No part of this publication may be reproduced,
stored in a retrieval system, or transmitted in any form or by
any means, electronic, mechanical, photocopying, recording
or otherwise, without the prior permission of the author.

This book is sold subject to the condition that it shall not, by way of
trade or otherwise, be lent, resold, hired out or otherwise circulated
without the author's prior consent in any form of binding or cover
other than that in which it is published and without a similar condition
including this condition being imposed on the subsequent purchaser.

YouCaxton Publications
enquiries@youcaxton.co.uk

For my fellow members of

The Scufflinks Golfing Society

Acknowledgements

I'd like to thank in particular two golfing companions who accompanied me on most of my visits covered in this book; Andrew Barr and my cousin, Neil Salvesen. Golf and whisky drinking are always more satisfying when experienced with others. Annoyingly, unlike me, both have recently improved their golf game. I think I will claim some credit for this.

The illustrations in this book are by Lara Brown, my eldest daughter, and Adam Katsoukis.

Contents

Acknowledgements — vi
Preface — ix

Chapter 1:   The Lake District   1
Chapter 2:   Yorkshire   15
Chapter 3:   East Anglia   33
Chapter 4:   Devon   47
Chapter 5:   Wales   65
Chapter 6:   Leinster   79
Chapter 7:   Ulster   95
Chapter 8:   Donegal   109
Chapter 9:   Kerry   125

Afterword — 139
Bibliography — 147

Preface

IN MY MORE melancholic moments, I have often compared life to a round of golf; full of highs and lows, fortune and misfortune, joys and frustrations and endless surprises. If I enjoy good health and complete four score years and ten, then I am currently putting out on the 12th green. My round started steadily in benign conditions and my first nine holes went very smoothly with me probably picking up at least two birdies. I was definitely better than par at the turn. Since then things have not gone so well; I have played some bad shots, had a number of (in my view) very unlucky bounces and given those shots back to par. Indeed as I putt out on the 12th my round is in danger of unravelling. But the beauty of golf is that if you put your mind to it, there is always the chance you can get the round back on track; a particularly good shot and a little bit of luck can make all the difference. So too with life.

One of the things that gives me hope that I can enjoy the rest of my life (round) is the prospect of visiting more beautiful golf courses as well as discovering interesting new whiskies. Being a proud Scot, I wanted to explore in my first book what it was about Scotland that enabled this small country to 'invent' two products or pastimes which are enjoyed by so many people around the world. I discovered that it was the mystery inherent in both that appeals so much, as this mystery and unfathomability in so many ways reflects life itself.

I chose to write nine chapters in that book always hoping that I would want to write a second which would represent, in golfing parlance, the 'back nine'. I initially considered nine further chapters in Scotland. There would be plenty of material; areas to which I had not gone, such as the Western Isles, Orkney, Arran, the Ayrshire coast, the Borders and Dumfries and Galloway. All now have activity in the whisky market and all, as everywhere in Scotland, have interesting golf courses. Indeed since writing the first book there has continued to be a huge amount of new activity in the Scotch whisky market with a further series of new openings and announcements of new ventures. It would be possible to do nine chapters on new openings alone. I can think of at least a dozen new distilleries since 2014 from Wolfburn in Thurso (which has become the mainland's most northerly distillery) to Ardnamurchan near Glenbeg (which has become the mainland's most westerly distillery) to Lone Wolf, a development from the successful micro-brewer, Brew Dog (this is situated in Ellon and so will become the mainland's most easterly distillery) to Annandale in Annan (which, until Bladnoch re-opens, will become the mainland's most southerly distillery). Also significant are a number of new island distilleries - Abhain Dearg on Lewis, the Harris Distillery, Torabhaig on Skye and R&B Distillers on Raasey. So, as you can see, there is activity the length and breadth of the country. And this investment is not just in smaller micro-distilleries; there are new distilleries being created by the big players. Diageo's Roseisle distillery in Moray, opened in 2009, has a capacity of 12.5 million litres, and Dalmunach, from Chivas Brothers, opened in 2015, has a capacity of 10 million litres, while the Edrington Group has invested in an architecturally innovative new distillery at Macallan to meet its growth ambitions for this famous Speyside brand. There would be plenty of potential to combine some of these sites with interesting golf courses; indeed the opening of a micro-distillery at the Castle Hotel in Dornoch is surely a perfect excuse to go back and play that wonderful course again.

But having learned what I did in Scotland, I think to explore both 'pastimes' more, I should move beyond Scotland and investigate how both are faring elsewhere. Golf soon spread from its beginnings in Scotland to the rest of the United Kingdom and Ireland and then to America in the late 19th century. Whisky, however, spread across the world to America and Japan in particular but within the United Kingdom was initially only produced in Ireland. Indeed, in the late 19th century the industry was as famous in Ireland as it was in Scotland, but it went into severe decline during the first half of the 20th century. I want to understand why this happened. For a long time there were only three distilleries remaining but gradually the industry has re-established its reputation and, over the past ten years in particular, there have been many new developments. England and Wales never had a whisky tradition but this is also changing and we are now seeing openings in a number of regions. I want to understand why this has taken so long. I am also keen to learn about whether golf is regarded differently across the country. Admittedly outside Scotland the link with whisky is much more tenuous and my locations will to an extent be driven by the location of the distilleries.

One of the marvels of my Scottish tour was that I visited not just nine beautiful golf courses and interesting distilleries but that there were so many wonderful locations. While the choice is more limited outside Scotland, I will use this as one of the criteria for where to visit. I have chosen four in England with quite a wide geographical spread, one in Wales, one in Northern Ireland and three in the Irish Republic. In England and Wales, I have deliberately chosen courses which have an association with Scotland (this is not difficult as so many of the great ones have this). In Ireland the courses have more of an Irish heritage, though, as I will explain, this heritage was heavily influenced, like its whiskey industry, by Scotland.

So what is the point of whisky outside Scotland? Is it just a poor relation? Irish whiskey (yes, it has an 'e' in Ireland) has a justifiable reputation, but will English or Welsh whisky ever match the reputation of the product produced by its famous neighbour? And is there the same passion for the product that you find north of the border?

It is worth remembering that Scotch is now a minnow in the world of whisky. The global market is dominated by Indian whisky though this is a very different product from either blended Scotch or Scotch malt whisky. Indeed the definition of whisky is an interesting point as Scotch is governed by fairly tight regulations whereas elsewhere in the world regulations are either much looser or non-existent. I will ponder whether this is a strength or a weakness for traditional Scotch as potentially it will allow new players distilling outside of Scotland to offer more innovative products. And the world of whisky is a growing one, with both the market growing and the number of new distilleries opening across the world increasing, and many countries developing a whisky industry; it is a bit like the wine industry where the established producers (France, Italy and Spain) have, over the past thirty years, faced increasing competition from 'New World' wines. 'New World' whiskies (which will also come from some 'Old World' countries such as France, Germany, Sweden and Austria) will undoubtedly play an increasingly important part in the market over the next thirty years. And the number of 'New World' producers will be much greater than for wine as the constraints of climate are not so significant. What will be interesting to see is, as many countries develop a whisky industry, whether particular countries can create a reputation for a distinctive product. How will Scotch fare against this rapidly increasing competition? As I visit England, Wales and Ireland it will be interesting to see how the new ventures will position themselves; how will they distinguish themselves from Scotch whisky, or do they see themselves as just part of a global trend with their geographical proximity to Scotland merely coincidental?

In golf it is also instructive to understand how the game changed as it moved south of the border which it did very quickly from the 1890s. While there are clearly more courses and golfers in England, golf does not have the same 'market share' of sport as it has in Scotland and the number of courses per head of population is much smaller. I mentioned in the last book that the Island of Arran with a population of about 5,000 people has seven golf courses; three with 18 holes, three with 9 holes and the famous 12 hole course at Shiskine. That's 93 golf holes on an island approximately 12 miles by 5 miles - it would be possible for 30 per cent of the entire population of Arran to play golf on the same day! In England there is much more competition from other sports while, as I mentioned in my first book, golf is facing some challenges in adapting to modern lifestyle trends. Put simply, it takes too long. Whisky, on the other hand, is becoming increasingly popular hence the distillery openings in England as well as across many other countries. However, this is mainly part of an artisan food and drink trend which is prevalent in a wide range of food and drink categories from cheeses, to breads, to beer and most recently spirits. And in spirits it is probably gin which is leading the way, as it can be brought more quickly to market and has, perhaps, a younger image. I will examine the influence of gin which is rapidly overtaking whisky in popularity. There is an increasing trend, also prevalent in Scotland, of producing whisky in a distillery alongside gin and vodka. The business advantages are clear but can this generalist approach ever produce the same passion for product quality of the focused whisky producer? Competition will not only come from the growing number of whisky producers but from gin and vodka and other spirits too.

This tour encompasses first, England and Wales, and then moves onto Ireland. We will start in The Lake District, move across to the east coast of Yorkshire, down to Norfolk and Suffolk and then to Devon in the West Country. Penderyn, Wales' most famous distillery, is handily placed near the south Pembrokeshire coast where the choice of golf courses is rich and from here it is easy to get the ferry from Fishguard to Ireland. The four distilleries which I have chosen in Ireland occupy almost the four corners of the island starting with the Dublin area, moving up to the Antrim coast in Northern Ireland, round to Donegal and then to County Kerry in the far south west. Arguably Ireland with, unlike England and Wales, its strong whiskey heritage, deserves more scrutiny but I will take the opportunity to examine that heritage, why the industry went into decline and is now booming, and the distinctiveness of Irish whiskey. Indeed it is a fascinating story with the tradition of Irish whiskey actually being rooted in premium malts, in contrast to the cheaper Scottish blends. In many ways the Scottish industry has now stolen the heritage of the Irish industry.

Finally, before embarking on this second tour, I must remind the reader that this is a book for amateur enthusiasts rather than experts. I am continually astonished at the number of books on whisky from extremely knowledgeable people. As I have said before, I am probably more discerning about my golf courses than my whiskies; this is, I think, because I have been playing golf for over fifty years yet drinking whisky for just about ten years. I am, however, keen to learn more but my comments on the product should be seen in this context. What I am learning is that there is always more to learn and that is one of the product's beauties. While arguably there is much less innovation in golf, there are also some interesting developments in course design and course upkeep which is generally improving the quality of experience. As soon as I finished my first book, while I had come to some conclusions, I had an uncontrollable thirst to discover and learn more. I hope that the same is true at the conclusion of this one.

CASTLEROCK
NARIN AND PORTNOO
BUSHMILLS
SLIABH LIAG
SILLOTH
THE LAKES
SPIRIT OF YORKSHIRE
GANTON
SLANE
THE ISLAND
THE ENGLISH WHISKY CO.
ROYAL WORLINGTON
CEANN SIBEAL
DINGLE
PENDERYN
PENNARD
WESTWARD HO!
DARTMOOR WHISKY

The first hole at Silloth

It is not a particularly demanding tee shot but you do
need to hit it straight. Heather borders each side of the
fairway making for a pretty outlook though if your ball
ends up in it you might not appreciate it so much.

CHAPTER ONE

The Lake District

'I wish to stimulate an interest in the art of distilling among those who trade in whisky, and to aid in demonstrating, what I am convinced is correct, that good whisky, as a beverage, is the most wholesome spirit in the world.'

Alfred Barnard (1837-1918)
The Whisky Distilleries of the United Kingdom

BARNARD'S MAGNIFICENT WORK, published in 1887, is not only incredibly comprehensive in its scope but also delightfully readable as we are invited to follow his journey which starts 'from Euston by night mail', with a visit to the Port Dundas Distillery in Glasgow, and ends on a 'Tram-car from Aldgate' to visit the Lea Valley Distillery in Stratford, London. While not in any way purporting to match the ambition of this extraordinary book, I will attempt to give structure to my own modest offering by describing some of the journeys between my chosen destinations as well as the places themselves.

As I finished my last book, 'my ninth hole', on the beautiful island of Islay, let us assume that we start this next tour from there and take the ferry back to the mainland, via Kennacraig and Arran, disembarking at Ardrossan on the Ayrshire coast. I feel a little guilty in travelling down this coast and ignoring a haven of golfing greatness from historic Prestwick to the now more famous Turnberry and many others. As we drive through the Southern Uplands into Dumfries and Galloway there are also two distilleries worth a visit: Bladnoch in Wigton has had a chequered history, had closed in 2014, but has since been bought by an Australian entrepreneur and has been re-opened, while in Annan close to the English border, the Annandale distillery is now flourishing. One golf course is also worth a mention and a visit: Southerness, situated south of Dumfries on the Solway Firth, was the first links course built after the Second World war by the famous architect Philip Mackenzie Ross (with Mackenzie and Ross in his name he was clearly destined from birth to become a golf course architect - Alister MacKenzie and Donald Ross being two of the early greats of golf course design). Mackenzie Ross was also responsible for rebuilding Turnberry much of which had been given over to an airfield during the war. Southerness sits on the delightful Solway estuary; it is classic 'linksland' though not a dramatic setting as there are no big dunes. The view is of the massive estuary with constant birdlife to watch and the hills of the Lake District in the distance. The course as a result is not memorable for its drama, more its clever, technical design with strategically placed bunkers and burns. Its attractions are more subtle than most; perhaps more like a mild lowland whisky than a peaty Islay variety. Mackenzie Ross was not as prolific a designer as many of his predecessors (partly because he followed the likes of Braid, Colt and Fowler and the market for new courses had reduced). His style, however, was very much in the naturalist tradition of MacKenzie and Colt and he was highly respected becoming the first President of the British Association of Golf Course Architects.

But we are headed out of Scotland, crossing the border at Gretna, and into the Lake District. It is the obvious place to start the next chapter in this tour. One of the worries about moving out of Scotland was whether I could find locations which matched the beauty and majesty of my chosen Scottish favourites. Clearly the Lake District is a match for any of the dramatically beautiful locations we visited in Scotland. I was therefore delighted that the opening of The Lakes Distillery enabled me to include this area while I already knew which course I wanted to include. In truth there is not a great deal of choice as the landscape of The Lake District is not conducive to there being many great golf courses. Even the coastline is relatively sparsely populated by golf courses compared to many other stretches in England. Perhaps Seascale, where there is an old links dating from 1893 designed by Willie Campbell (who designed the original Machrie course on Islay), would have been a candidate, but it does not compete with Silloth, which I had visited a number of years ago and knew would fit all my rigorous criteria for inclusion in the book.

Silloth-on-Solway, to give it its full name, is an attractive small seaside town with a cobbled High Street. It also boasts a three mile long sea promenade and a working harbour most famous for its Solway brown shrimps. At the southern end of the town there is also a flour mill which is a useful guide to the golf course entrance. The charming old clubhouse with its red roof sits up from the car park and looks directly out onto the course. It dates from 1903, is full of character and has plenty of history. There are pictures of many of its famous members such as Willie Whitelaw, Mrs Thatcher's Deputy Prime Minister and a local MP in the area, who was Captain of the club back in 1970 and then became President until his death in 1999. Whitelaw was a very keen golfer and a past R&A Captain. Perhaps the most prominent portrait, however, is of Cecilia Leitch, one of the most famous early lady golfers. Cecilia, known as Cecil, was born in Silloth one of seven children, won four Ladies Amateur Championships and five French titles and was regarded as one of the world's top lady golfers of her day. Her battles with Joyce Wethered did much to advance the profile and popularity of the women's game in the United Kingdom. Two of her sisters were also successful golfers.

The club was founded in 1892 by the North British Railway Company which was keen to develop Silloth as a holiday destination. Well known designers such as Willie Fernie and Willie Park were consulted on the course design though neither lay claim to its overall layout which was undertaken by the less well known Scottish golfer Davie Grant. Alister Mackenzie is also later credited with improvements so it has some real pedigree.

If Southerness' charms are of the subtle, understated variety, Sillloth's are more obvious from very early in the round. The first hole plays straight out along a pleasant, but not over-generous, fairway lined by heather. You cannot see the green, not even from where you play your second, but there is a marker post. The reason you can't is that the fairway suddenly plunges down to a hidden green delightfully situated in a small dell. The second hole is a crafty dog-leg which, by contrast, you can see in its entirety from the lofted tee. Don't play too straight or you will run out of space but don't also try and cut off too much of the corner or you will leave yourself a tricky second to what is quite a small green. The third is another dog-leg (this time right to left) with the second playing up to a precariously situated plateau green. The fourth heads back towards the clubhouse while the fifth is a wonderful long Par 5 which plays along a narrow fairway beside the sea. The fifth, the first of the Par 3s, is played inland and then there are further interesting holes amidst the dunes before you reach the 9th which is a very short Par 3, facing out into the Irish Sea, and appropriately called 'The Manx' as on a clear day you can see the Isle of Man. I have played this hole three times and, while it is only about 120 yards, I have used three different clubs; a 9 iron, a 6 iron and a 4 iron. It is the most exposed point on the course and the wind is a huge factor.

Cecilia Leitch

The 10th hole takes you a little further out before the 11th starts the return home. Again on the back 9 all the holes are interesting. The two Par 3s are slightly longer than those on the front 9 though will usually have the prevailing wind behind.

The toughest hole is definitely the first of two consecutive Par 5s, the 13th, which plays back away from the clubhouse. It is not long for a Par 5 though likely to be into the prevailing wind and the second shot is uphill through a narrow gully to an elevated ridge which falls away steeply both sides. While the third shot to the green should be relatively short, miss it at your peril. The 14th is another interesting Par 5 though generally easier despite a blind second. The 17th is the third Par 5 on the back 9 before you reach the final hole which is called 'The Whitelaw' in memory of the club's famous past President.

Silloth is a delightful course; a classic links in good condition with quality holes and a touch of old fashioned quirkiness which makes it distinctive and memorable. As there are some blind shots there are a number of posts with red metal bells to be struck to signal to players behind that it is safe to play - it all adds to the character. Silloth is more interesting than just another links course. It also scores on location as the Solway Firth, which it overlooks, is beautiful while the mountains of the Lake District give it context on the landward side.

Silloth often appears either top of or very near the top of lists of 'best value' golf courses. This is understandable as the green fees for a course of this quality remain very modest while membership subscriptions are also incredibly good value. I also remember on my first visit many years ago having a very enjoyable lunch in the clubhouse of soup and cottage pie with chips and peas. Modest fare, yes, but good and honest. There were four of us and I went to pay the bill, asking how much I owed. '£20' I was told. My immediate instinct was that this was surprisingly steep; I suppose a fiver for the soup, which had admittedly been accompanied by a roll, and fifteen quid for the pie with chips and vegetables was not out of the ordinary. I was at that time working in the south of England and had corporate membership at Wentworth where such prices were commonplace but I was not expecting it at Silloth. It was only when I started rummaging in my wallet that I realised that it was actually £20 for all four of us! Yes, a fiver EACH.

The drive to The Lakes Distillery on Bassenthwaite is only about 40 minutes and the scenery gets more beautiful the closer you get. The distillery is the brainchild of Paul Currie who with his father, a previous Managing Director of Chivas Seagram, set up the Arran Distillery in 1995. It has been a big project as The Lakes is not just a small micro-distillery set up in a disused farm building in the Lake District; it is a big business encompassing a visitor centre, shop and a bistro while significant investment has been put into restoring the old buildings in a sensitive rural area. There is now a Head Office in Newcastle and the business announced in late 2018 that it intended to float on the AIM market.

Paul teamed up with Nigel Mills as Chairman, a local businessman and owner of the Trout Inn in Cockermouth, and brought in a former Diageo production director and an operations director from Macallan, so there is no shortage of whisky expertise. Similar hirings were made for the bistro and hospitality side of the business. It is immediately apparent on your arrival that there has been a lot of investment. While the scale is relatively small, the quality of experience is in line with what you would get at, for example, Glenmorangie or Ardbeg. The setting is also delightful, at northern end of Bassenthwaite on the River Derwent at the top end of The Lake District, which in 2017 became a World Heritage Site.

The setting is important in many respects. The Lake District, being situated within two hours of the major conurbations of the north west of England, is one of the most popular tourist areas in the country and the business model of 'The Lakes' relies on more than just selling whisky. The visitor centre, shop and bistro are an important part of the business and rely on visitor numbers which are even now impressive to the extent that it has already become one of the most visited distilleries in the whole of the UK. It is designed for a day out - distillery visit, refreshments in the bistro, a browse around the well-stocked shop, even a delightful walk down to the River Derwent where you can talk to a herd (I think that is the correct collective noun) of alpacas which is kept in the neighbouring field.

The buildings were an old Victorian dairy farm dating from the 1860s which had stood empty for 20 years. They have been sympathetically restored with local stone and slate while incorporating modern technology such as a biomass boiler, photo voltaic cells and wool insulation to make the whole site as 'green' as possible. The building, as was typical of the time, also had distinctive architectural features, in particular numerous 'quatrefoils', a four leafed clover mark, which they have not only maintained in the new buildings but have commandeered as a marketing proposition for the new distillery. The four leaves were originally supposed to represent the four Gospels but became secularised to represent Faith, Hope, Luck and Love and they have taken these values to embody the story of the setting up of the new distillery. You can buy a very smartly produced book in the shop which tells the story of the founding of the distillery using this theme.

The site is well designed for visitors with tours every hour and the bistro selling drinks, snacks and meals. It is always a problem for a distillery to decide how to make a tour distinctive and 'worth the money'. The basic tour is relatively expensive at £12.50 but you certainly get your money's worth with a professionally presented story including lots of local history as well as the usual explanation of the whisky and gin making processes. Everything inside looks well maintained and it is interesting to see the different stills for whisky and gin. The storage is also onsite in an old cattle shed which has been appropriately transformed. The main feature of the tour, however, is a spectacular film which follows helicopter footage of the distillery's precious water source, the River Derwent. The film follows the river from its source close to Styhead Tarn near the famous Scafell Pike (an area reputed to have one of the highest levels of rainfall in England) down Borrowdale, through Bassenthwaite, past the distillery and then through the Isel Valley where at Cockermouth it meets up with the River Cocker before reaching the coast at Workington from where it flows into the Solway Firth. The tour is worth it for watching this video alone.

So what about the product? The first malt whisky was released as a 3 year old in 2018. Just 101 bottles were released of *Genesis*, a cask strength whisky matured first in oloroso hogsheads and then American and European oak and finished in Spanish wine casks. It's an exotic mix for a three year old whisky. For the uninitiated it is quite confusing as they already sell a brand called The One, which is in fact a 'British' blend of whiskies produced across the British Isles. Effectively this has nothing to do with the Lakes except it enables them to sell whisky while they are waiting for their own spirit to mature and at about £30 a bottle is a rather expensive blend. But it would be wrong to criticise; it makes good sense for the cash flow and likewise the well-stocked shop also sells a wide range of gins and many other items. It is a well-tuned marketing operation and if the business is to be successful, it needs to be. More recently they have produced a blended malt called Steel Bonnets which blends their own malt with a Scotch malt.

My sense is that their whisky will look to be distinctive. Being an English whisky it is not governed by the strict Scotch Whisky regulations and the area which interests the Lakes most is the use of different barrels in which to mature the spirit as is reflected in the Genesis product. Scotch whisky has to be matured in oak and initially the Lakes planned to experiment with the likes of cedar and maple. Yet, these are whisky people so I am sure that quality will be the primary focus and innovation of this sort will only be undertaken if it produces a genuinely interesting and good quality end product. There will be important decisions to take, such as what will be their mainstream malt line (presumably a Non-Age statement expression) and how they will produce different expressions in different woods. Scotch whisky is restricted to oak but clearly the barrels can have been used for different purposes; bourbon, sherry, brandy etc. What different woods might contribute will be interesting to see.

It's time to talk again about gin. The Lakes is producing gin using a separate still and it is an important part of their portfolio. Beyond the obvious cash flow benefits of not having to wait three years to have product to sell, they can clearly see benefits of having gin as part of their product portfolio. There are a number of different varieties (as well as sloe, damson and elderflower gin liqueurs) and they give it a 'Cumbrian' provenance by using 'local botanicals'. But to what extent is it a competitor to whisky? There is growth in new whiskies but it is dwarfed by the growth in new gins. The number of new gin distilleries doubled between 2012 and 2017 to over 300, with 49 opening in 2017 alone. Gin continues to gain market share or 'share of throat' as the industry experts would describe it. Yet gin is much easier to make so the quality is inevitably more variable. Small batch or small scale does not necessarily mean good quality; indeed sometimes quite the opposite. In fact gin does not even have to be distilled as some gins are made by a process called 'cold compounding' which effectively means infusing neutral spirit (which can be bought in bulk) with flavours. There are some small producers who claim this process can produce a quality gin but it is generally associated with cheaper products. But even distilled gin can be made cheaply with raw spirit bought in batches and then re-distilled through a pot still which can be sourced cheaply on the internet and installed in a garage. So beware the artisan gin maker. Do your research into the product.

Gin's image is also very different. Gin is something of a young, brash upstart to whisky's serious, mature personality. You drink gin and sip whisky. Gin satisfies a thirst; whisky satisfies the mood and the soul. I sense a degree of 'fad' with the number of new gin launches. There will be new gins which position themselves as traditional and serious and there may be some whiskies that look to be young and edgy, but these will be the exceptions. Whisky is more than a humble drink just as golf is more than just another sport.

Diageo, the biggest UK whisky company, a few years ago

introduced a new brand called Haig Club. This is a clever marketing exercise in many ways. Haig is a very traditional whisky brand; many may remember the famous 'Dimple' bottle. The product is a 'single grain' whisky so can be produced relatively cheaply in high volumes but the 'single' statement gives a quality signal. The packaging is smart using a fresh looking, distinctively shaped, blue bottle. The advertising features David Beckham. The website suggests mixing it with sparkling apple soda (somehow I'm not sure I would add that to a 25 year-old Glenlivet). I am not criticising. It is aimed at quite a different market. It is looking to attract a younger audience to whisky. It is the cricket equivalent of Twenty20 to malt whisky's 5-day test match. It is effectively a cocktail base and whisky has a tradition of being used in many famous cocktails. But as a drink it is as far away from a malt whisky as a gin or a vodka.

I've talked about golf's need to move with the times and attract a younger audience. I think this can be done without sacrificing the essential character of the sport. Relaxing fussy dress codes, reforming esoteric rules and organising shorter competition formats all make sense and can be done without damaging the essential spirit of the sport.

The Lakes is a model for the 'new world' whisky industry. It is founded on the traditions of the industry but will take the opportunity to innovate. As we progress the tour around these new whisky distilleries in England, it will be interesting to see what approach is taken to the product. As more distilleries are developed in England, the 'Englishness' itself will not be enough. In Scotland, the regional designations (e.g. Highland, Speyside, Lowland etc.) help give a brand a sense of identity. In England, where currently there is no 'English Whisky

Association', this does not exist. Ultimately, as in any food or drink market, the quality of the product will be crucial. Here I can claim some expertise: I have spent my career in food marketing and I can tell you that good branding, design and marketing is a fundamental part of the success of any food or drink product, but good branding, design and marketing cannot ultimately make a poor orordinary product successful. That is my free consultancy advice to all the new whisky start-ups. From my experience, most do not need to be told this, though perhaps it is a danger with some of the numerous new gins now available.

CHAPTER TWO

Yorkshire

'The object of a bunker or trap is not only to punish a physical mistake, to punish lack of control, but to punish pride and egotism'

Charles Blair MacDonald (1855-1939)
Winner of the first US Amateur and designer of the first 18-hole golf course in the US

I WANTED MY choice of regions in England to give as wide a geographical spread as possible. Where to go was inevitably dictated by the location of whisky distilleries; while there are golf courses nearly everywhere even in England, whisky distilleries are still relatively rare. In the north of England, Lancashire has a coastline rich in great golf courses but at the time of writing there are no signs of any whisky production. I read of plans for a distillery in Wooller near the Scottish border in Northumberland. But I was delighted to discover distilleries opening in Yorkshire, as somehow I think any tour of England should include Yorkshire. I may be biased as I have Yorkshire connections; my mother was from Yorkshire (though her mother was a Scot) and I have many happy childhood memories visiting my grandparents in Yorkshire and I still have family living there. So while I have lived in the south of England for over thirty years, I feel that Yorkshire is my spiritual English home. I enthusiastically support Yorkshire at cricket- perhaps that says it all. My grandfather took me to my first test match at Headingley and Geoffrey Boycott was a sporting hero. I also think that there is something about Yorkshire that fits with whisky; it's a county with a real sense of pride, whose people have a 'no nonsense' approach to life and generally adhere to timeless values as opposed to passing fads. Yorkshire has also much to be proud of; everyone will remember when Yorkshire representatives of the British Olympic Team (I have always found the term 'Team GB' slightly irritating) had significant successes in the 2012 Olympic Games to the extent that the Yorkshire media produced a medals table showing Yorkshire ahead of both Germany and Australia. This was done with the tongue firmly in the cheek but it also made a point. I like that.

There was a choice of two distilleries: Cooper King near York and the Spirit of Yorkshire in Hunmanby at the north end of the Yorkshire Wolds. The choice for me was relatively easy as the latter was just fifteen minutes from Ganton Golf Club which I knew had an interesting history but which I had never played. The Hunmanby distillery was also, unlike Cooper King - which is leading with gin - a whisky focused operation.

To reach Ganton from The Lakes you head down the M6 and turn off along the A66, a delightful road across the Yorkshire Dales that takes you over to the A1 which you join at Scotch Corner. From there you can head south down the A1 and turn off through Thirsk and up the precipitous Sutton Bank onto the North York Moors and through the delightful towns of Helmsley, Kirbymoorside and Pickering. This journey encompasses all the best of Yorkshire so take time to enjoy its delights.

Ganton lies at the point where the Yorkshire Wolds end and the Yorkshire Moors start. To the south it has views of the Wolds and to the north of the Moors, so the scenery is delightful, though on some holes around the turn, the setting is not quite as peaceful as it might be because it neighbours the busy A64 road from York to Scarborough. It is an inland course (it is just under 10 miles as the crow flies to the coast at either Scarborough or Filey) but on arriving you could be forgiven for thinking it is a links as you can see huge swathes of sand and what look like dunes. Thinking it was near the North York Moors I had expected a more heathland feel but Ganton is different.

The iconic wrought iron gates at The Lakes Distillery

Indeed playing Ganton has made me reappraise my view that 'most of the best courses are links courses'. The issue is not whether it is 'links' in the true sense of being land originally reclaimed from the sea (though potentially Ganton, if you go back tens of thousands of years, may have been by the sea). What I now realise is that the kind of golf I like is played on sandy soil with fine grasses and whether that sand or turf is by the sea or not is irrelevant. There is an excellent book by the golf course designer George Waters, called *Sand and Golf*, which explains this and it was playing at Ganton and reading his book that brought it home to me. It is sandy terrain which delivers the subtlety to the game and sandy terrain does not need to be by the sea. He mentions Sand Hills in Nebraska (not at all near the sea) and the famous sand belt courses in Melbourne such as Royal Melbourne and Kingston Heath. And of course it is the sandy characteristics of heathland courses which make them so special. Sandy courses are generally more 'natural' and also generally require less maintenance and are therefore ecologically better.

If there is one word which describes Ganton, one word which defines its uniqueness, it has to be 'bunkers'. I thought that I had seen big bunkers but nowhere have I seen so many big bunkers as at Ganton. And some are bigger than big. And by 'big', I don't just mean their width and length. These are not huge expanses of American-style shallow fairway bunkers; these are proper, deep bunkers as well. If you were to measure the cubic capacity of the bunkers, I can't believe that there is a course in the world with more 'bunkerage' than Ganton. They are monsters. Think Hell Bunker at St Andrews and the enormously deep cross bunkers on the 17th at Muirfield and then multiply this across nearly all of the 18 holes. Also the natural terrain means that the catchment area for these bunkers is even larger as balls gather towards them. There are also interesting design features; on the 6th and the 15th there are large fairway bunkers (on the right of the 6th and the left of the 15th) where the bunkers are twenty to thirty yards long. On most bunkers the carry from front to back may be 5 – 10 yards. Here it is 20-30 yards!

Playing Ganton brought home to me what proper golf is all about. It should be a subtle and thinking game and not a mechanical one. I scored terribly the first time I played it. I am a mid-handicapper (10-11) and my score was probably only just in two figures. But actually it was not my swing that was wrong; it was that I played unintelligently, and when you play unintelligently surrounded by these enormous bunkers, you will suffer accordingly.

Let me explain. Ganton has quite a lot of long Par 4s. It was windy so many were a stretch for a golfer like me who does not hit the ball that far. Often on a Par 4 my second shot to the green would be anywhere between 180-220 yards. What club to play? A 4 iron? A rescue club? Or perhaps a 3 wood, depending on the wind. Of course the answer for a mid-handicapper like me is actually none of these. The answer was probably 'two 9 irons'. So often I forgot that I actually have a handicap of 11 and the likelihood of me threading a 3 wood 200 yards into the wind onto the green between cavernous bunkers is pretty low. Why was it that I only realised this when contemplating my round later that evening over a malt whisky?

The truth is that I generally scored better when I hit a poorer drive and was forced to lay up with my second safely away from the bunkers. Then a pitch on to the green and two putts for a five. But a five at a long par 4 for an eleven handicap player is actually quite respectable.

This is why matchplay golf is so good. It forces you to think more sensibly. It will also change what is the right shot to play. Sometimes you will need to make a four so the right shot is to go for the green. But if a five is enough it would be daft to go for the green and risk a 6. So in matchplay golf you can't adopt one strategy for the whole round – each shot on each hole needs thinking about. It sometimes encourages high risk golf and other times favours safety play. It is perhaps why the Ryder Cup is such a popular golf event to watch. I know of many people who week in and week out will not watch golf but will watch The Ryder Cup. I know of football fanatics who will still quote the Ryder Cup as their favourite sporting event. It is no coincidence that it produces exciting golf – that is what the matchplay format does and it is why I think both the professional golf authorities and the clubs should encourage more matchplay tournaments.

Ganton is an excellent example of a strategic design. There is an interesting section in *Sand and Golf* which George Waters calls 'Too much information'. Many golfers nowadays obsess about which club to play and believe that the main factor in the decision is knowing precisely how far it is to the flag. The popularity of GPS distance devices is evidence of this. These have been allowed by the R&A on the basis that they should speed up play. I'm not so sure. For me discreet 100 and 150 yard markers, plus maybe distances on sprinkler heads are a good thing. I worry about the binocular ones which seem to take quite a lot of time to register. I have also known different players in my fourball pronounce very different distances having looked through their respective devices leading to further review and debate. And the truth is that for most golfers - indeed, all but the very top players - it is probably the least important factor in the ensuing shot. Yes, you need to know an approximate distance. Frequently I have approached my ball on the fairway, looked across and mumbled, 'So, about 155 yards'. My playing companion, eager to show off his or her new device, will authoritatively pronounce, '159 to the pin'.

Oh! That changes everything. Er, no it doesn't. What is much more important is the lie of the land, the likely hardness of the bounce, whether you are going to hit it high or low and crucially how well you hit it. Deciding whether it is a 5 or a 6 iron is usually the least of your problems yet the amount of time many people spend worrying about this is extraordinary. I've seen people using distance devices when they are about 30 yards from the green. What is it telling them? And what do they do with the information?

I should apologise to non-golfers here for this slight rant. But I think it reflects on modern life generally. Harry Vardon and Ted Ray, two famous sons of Ganton, seemed to manage without distance devices. Indeed Ray had no time for anything that slowed up play; 'to think, when we ought to play, is madness' he once said. Frequently modern technology can be clever but not useful. I admit that my golf game is probably less technical than that of many others. I have not had a lesson in 45 years which is perhaps why I have never had a low handicap. But I think golf is more enjoyable when it is not played by numbers. When I stand over a shot, the right type of shot generally comes to mind. One of the factors will be the distance, but only one. It is generally what feels right and if it feels right you will more than likely play the right shot.

So while I played Ganton for the very first time badly, I loved it. That probably disproves my theory that people generally like courses where they have played well. So I will call Ganton the exception which proves the rule and I plan to return and play it better next time. What else is there to say about Ganton? As well as bunkers there is quite a lot of gorse, so again accurate play is required. Obviously the turf is good and the direction of the holes changes frequently as the round progresses so judging the wind is always a factor. There is a good mix of hole lengths with some good short Par 4s; the 14th perhaps the most noteworthy, requiring an accurate lay up short of the bunkers on a slight dog-leg. The finish is also worth a mention. 16 is a long Par 4 with a tightish drive over a large cross bunker and then a second along a narrow but gathering fairway to a green inevitably guarded by tricky bunkers. 17 then plays across the entrance road and is either a long Par 3 or a short Par 4 depending on which tee is used. It is actually an excellent example of what Alister MacKenzie regarded as a good hole. It looks more fearsome than it is. From the tee, it is not clear where you can safely land the ball. In fact there is a generous area short of the green which will reward a straight shot. Anything not straight, however, will almost inevitably find one of a number of difficult bunkers. 18 is then a dog leg left with the second shot playing back across the road to a slightly elevated green in front of the clubhouse.

The clubhouse is an attractive old building with pleasant well-kept gardens in front of it. The inside has been modernised but its proud history is well displayed. The course was first laid out in 1891 by Tom Chisholm from St Andrews. The site was probably influenced by the railway line as Ganton Halt was just a few hundred yards away. In 1896 Harry Vardon became the professional and while he was there he won the first three of his Open Championship victories as well as the US Open in 1900. Vardon was then succeeded by his friend Ted Ray who, along with Vardon, was one of only six British players who have won both the The Open and the US Open. During Ray's tenure as professional there was a major redesign of the course in conjunction with Vardon and his fellow 'triumvirate' members, James Braid and J H Taylor. Subsequently Colt, MacKenzie and Tom Simpson were all, at different times, hired to make improvements so the course's design pedigree is second to none. It is not surprising therefore that the course has held many famous tournaments. It is the only course to have held the Ryder Cup (1949), the Curtis Cup (2000) and the Walker Cup (2003) and is the only inland course to have held the Amateur Championship (1964 and 1977). In addition it has held many other prestigious amateur tournaments.

It is worth reminding ourselves of who Vardon and Ray were. They were both born in Jersey and were golfing superstars of their time. Vardon won The Open six times between 1896 and 1914 and was runner up a further four times. In the 20 years before the Great War either Vardon, Braid or Taylor won 16 times (Ray won one of the four they didn't with Vardon runner up and one of the three was runner up in each of the other years they didn't win). When they competed in the US Open, which was obviously less frequently, they also did well. When Vardon won in 1900, Taylor was runner up. When Ray won in 1920, Vardon was runner-up. Vardon and Ray, however, are probably best remembered for the 1913 US Open when they were defeated in a play-off by the unknown local boy, Francis Ouimet, a story beautifully told in the book *The Greatest Game Ever Played* by Mark Frost. Ouimet's against-the-odds victory was credited with the start of the golf boom in America which took off after the end of the war.

Vardon was undoubtedly the greatest golfer of his time. He was one of the first major players to use the overlapping grip, which became known as the 'Vardon grip'. His strength was his accuracy, with putting a relative weakness and there is evidence that in his later years he got the dreaded putting yips. Ray's strength by contrast was the prodigious distances he could hit the ball. A tall man, usually sporting a trilby hat with a pipe clenched between his teeth, he was not the most accurate of players but had, by necessity, a good recovery game. He also played at pace; he would not have understood how modern players take four hours plus to play a round.

There is a Vardon Room in the clubhouse with many old pictures of these golfing greats. The pictures of the course are also revealing, showing quite a raw and barren landscape. I like it when clubs display historical artefacts – we will see this at each of our next two visits. There should be pride in a club's history and it makes sense for clubs to make the most of this. At Royal Wimbledon, one of England's older clubs, they recently found a lot of archive material hidden away and have now converted one of their lovely clubhouse rooms into a museum. There is also a fascinating museum at Royal Blackheath which is England's oldest club (not course). It makes me think that clubs which I visited in *Of Peats and Putts* could do more; Bora could have a 'mini museum' on Braid; Tain and Moray on Old Tom Morris.

One of the most interesting pictures is of Harry Vardon's clubs. These are named as follows: *Driver, Brassie, Driving Cleek, Light Cleek, Driving Mashie, Iron, Mashie, Niblick and*

Putter. I much prefer these names to just 5 iron or 7 iron. I also like the fact that there are only 9. I'm sure this helped them play more quickly and more instinctively. Francis Ouimet allegedly won the US Open in 1913 with just 7. Alister MacKenzie, in his book *The Spirit of St Andrews*, suggested the rules of golf should restrict a player to just six clubs citing how John Ball, winner of eight Amateur Championships, rarely used that many. In many ways the game must have been more innately skilful. I sometimes wonder whether mid-handicap golfers are helped or hindered by having as many as 14 clubs. It creates doubt. At our club we have an annual '3 clubs and a putter' competition – my regular foursomes partner's best ever round was when he won this tournament. Instead of creating doubt, it clears the mind. Incidentally, the rule limiting the number of clubs to 14 was not introduced until 1938 perhaps in response to Lawson Little who won the Amateur Championship in 1934 with 31 clubs!

The Spirit of Yorkshire Distillery is situated on the edge of a new industrial estate on the outskirts of the small town of Hunmanby, about eight miles from Ganton. Hunmanby is a pretty little town with just one main street and an attractive church. Unlike The Lakes Distillery or most of my chosen Scottish ones, I can't claim the location of the distillery is beautiful though the surrounding countryside is pleasant. The site is, however, smartly presented as it is has a visitor centre, shop and café which have attracted a considerable number of visitors.

The enterprise was set up by two local entrepreneurs and works in partnership with The Wolds Brewery, a microbrewery set up a few miles away in 2003 by the third and fourth generation of a family of arable farmers. In fact the distillery only distils – it gets its 'mash' from the brewery so only part of the process is on site. We will also see this in Devon in Chapter 4. It means that the whole focus on this distillery site is on the actual distilling. The company brand uses a gannet as its logo. A video explains that this is to reflect the business's pride in its locality with nearby Bempton Cliffs being the largest gannet colony on the UK mainland. (I initially questioned this as I had always thought the famous Bass Rock off North Berwick was the UK's largest gannet colony – in fact it is, but Bempton Cliffs is the largest *mainland* one.)

However, the relevance of the location is less about the gannets and more about the barley. In many ways this is an obvious place to build a distillery. The Yorkshire Wolds are one of the main areas for growing malting barley in the UK and Muntons Maltings at Flamborough, just down the coast, is one of the country's biggest suppliers of malted barley to the Scotch whisky industry. This means that the main raw material, unlike at many Scottish distilleries nowadays, is genuinely local so there is a good business reason for building a distillery in this part of Yorkshire.

I was impressed, however, that the Spirit of Yorkshire is not just relying on its Yorkshire provenance for its differentiation. The single focus on distilling has led them to innovate as they have not only two Forsyths pot stills (they claim that they were lucky to get these quickly, jumping the queue as 'Brexit uncertainty' had put other orders on hold) but also a four plate copper column still which they will use in tandem with the traditional pot stills. They fervently believe that there is value and differentiation to be gained from tweaking the distilling process. I am not enough of an expert to comment but it is encouraging to see a new business exploring these options. The business had worked with one of the industry's foremost distilling experts, Dr Jim Swan. Swan, a Fellow of the Royal Society of Chemistry, became a leading light in The Scotch Whisky Research Institute undertaking pioneering research into the whisky production process and the effects of maturation in particular. In the last 15 years of his life (he died suddenly in 2017), he operated as an independent consultant, renowned around the world, undertaking work for a number of new distilleries from Kilchoman and Penderyn in the UK to Kavalan in Thailand and others in Canada, Israel and India. It would be fair to say that he was as well known in the whisky industry in the early years of the 21st century as Harry Vardon was within golfing circles one hundred years earlier. Indeed his international reputation reminds me of the famous Scottish course designers who left Scotland in the late 19th and early 20th century to design courses in the United States; Donald Ross, Willie Park Junior, Willie Anderson and many others. Just as Scotland then had the reputation for golf course design expertise which so many in the 'New World' wanted to emulate, so too did Swan with his Scottish background, skills and expertise. While 'whisky' has been produced all over the world for a long time, Scotch malt whisky still has the reputation for being the ultimate premium expression of proper whisky. Kavalan acknowledge on their website the contribution made by Dr Swan to the success of their product.

At the time of writing, The Spirit of Yorkshire has not yet produced whisky as the first distilling was only began in 2016, so the case for their unique distilling process remains unproven.

Their plans on maturation are more mainstream, focusing on first fill ex-bourbon casks as well as sherry and red wine. But there is another fascinating innovation which this distillery has introduced. We have previously come across start-up distilleries selling gin to generate cash or bottling another distillery's spirit to gain sales while they wait the three years (at least) for their whisky to mature. The Lakes Distillery is a good example with their wide range of gins and the blended whisky 'The One' which really has nothing to do with the distillery. The Spirit of Yorkshire has thought laterally and has released limited quantities of what they call 'maturing malt'; i.e. whisky which isn't yet whisky. They apparently had quite a difficult time with trading standards officers so the word whisky doesn't appear on the bottle. The official product description is 'distilled spirit' but they managed to persuade trading standards for that to be written on the back of the label with the rather more appealing 'maturing malt' appearing on the front.

And what is interesting is that this 'very young whisky' really is lovely to drink. Even after just over a year, its character is taking shape and as they have experimented with a range of barrels the differences are already clear. It's a clever approach and one which I'm sure others will consider. Clearly it will only ever involve limited quantities as longer term they have no incentive to sell too much as it would reduce potential stocks of real whisky in the future.

I tried all three expressions which they had released in their first two years (they helpfully allow car drivers who have taken their distillery tour to take away samples in tiny tasting bottles) and could clearly tell the differences between them. Perhaps they are quite light and lacking in real depth and complexity.

Or is that because I know that they are young? And again, was it me, or did I find the spirit very clean and pure? Could that be the result of the very sophisticated distilling process?

The visitor centre has an extremely good coffee shop called The Pot Still. In fact it is rather more than a 'coffee shop' as it sells lunches and a range of snacks throughout the day. It is also the location for a number of distillery events. As well as occasional special tours they have jazz and music evenings all designed to create awareness of the brand and bring in cash flow as the precious stock matures before it can be released for sale as 'whisky'. With a combination of knowledgeable and passionate people, some interesting differentiated approaches to whisky making and a developing brand based on their Yorkshire provenance, The Spirit of Yorkshire is well placed amongst the English newcomers to make its mark.

YORKSHIRE

One of Ganton's many bunkers

This example is less cavernous than some though it has all the distinctive features such as the use of railway sleepers to reinforce the sides plus small steps marking the entry point. Keeping them well raked and in a tidy condition must be a major challenge for the green keeping staff.

.

The Pink Jug

'Lemon, ice, champagne and equal tots of
Benedictine, brandy and Pimms No.1'

The origin of the drink dates from 1934 when a Royal Worlington member held a party on two consecutive days. When he found that most of the drink had been consumed on the first day, he decided to make up a cocktail with what was left. I have to confess that I have never tasted it but it does sound rather good.

CHAPTER THREE

East Anglia

*'For this game, above all things, you need
to be in a tranquil frame of mind'*

Harry Vardon (1870-1937)
Six time winner of The Open Championship

My next location is where the recent renaissance of the English whisky industry began. In 2006, planning permission was granted at a site in Roudham, Norfolk, for a new whisky distillery which was to become the first in England for over 100 years. I use the word 'renaissance' because, while whisky was generally regarded as an industry focused in Scotland and Ireland in the 19th century, there were actually a few English distilleries. Alfred Barnard, in his book of 1887, mentions four; two in Liverpool, one in Bristol and probably the most famous at Lea Valley in London which was owned by the Distillers Company, the forerunner of today's market leader, Diageo.

There are now other options in the south east of England; in London, The London Distillery Company has two sites in Battersea and Bermondsey, while Copper Rivet in Chatham and Bimber in Park Royal, which were initially gin and vodka producers, also now produce whisky. The original 'London Distillery Company' was the one in Lea Valley which had been founded as early as 1807 by an entrepreneur and the new venture is looking to embody similar values of innovation and distinctiveness. It is very much a craft operation. While I have nothing against Battersea and Bermondsey, these locations counted against it featuring in this book. Adnams, the famous brewer, has also added a distillery to its brewery in Southwold, Suffolk, which is a very beautiful location with plenty of nearby golfing options but as the new distillery is effectively just an offshoot of a major beer brand, it didn't seem right. The St George's Distillery at Roudham, by contrast, deserves its place as the pioneer of the new interest in English whisky.

There are of course many great courses in the south east of England though perhaps Norfolk, with its flat landscape, is not the most renowned area. The best are the links courses on the north Norfolk coast at Hunstanton and Brancaster. I have chosen, however, to go just across the border into Suffolk to what is often regarded as the best 9 hole course in the UK - Royal Worlington. It is quite an eccentric course in many ways but, as you will have by now realised, I cherish eccentricity, especially in golf courses.

I can't claim that the landscapes around either the distillery at Roudham or Royal Worlington (they are about half an hour apart) are dramatically beautiful. Indeed I am not a great fan of the landscape in East Anglia. I was brought up in the Borders of Scotland and have lived most of my life in the Chilterns so am used to having hills around me. I think hills are important both to contextualise a landscape and also provide long views. You seldom get this in Norfolk in particular. I spent three years at university in Cambridge and did feel the flatness of the landscape there. Somehow I find being surrounded by hills gives a sense of security. An alternative to having hills is seeing the coastline; again it gives context.

However, if neither the setting at Roudham nor Royal Worlington can compete with Islay or The Lake District they are both very pleasant and quite peaceful. Royal Worlington is situated at Mildenhall just off the A11 a few miles north of Newmarket. Newmarket is worth a visit especially for its newly and extravagantly refurbished horseracing museum which is in the centre of the small town. More properly called 'The National Heritage Centre for Horseracing and Sporting Art', it is situated at Palace House which along with neighbouring buildings has been carefully restored. Royal connections go back to James I (James VI of Scotland of course) who first built a palace at Newmarket though the site which has been restored was actually built by Charles II in 1671. You do not have to be a racing enthusiast to enjoy a visit either to the buildings or the museum. There is also a very good restaurant.

You approach Royal Worlington along a fairly anonymous road and come across the clubhouse to your right sitting in front of a putting green with a car park to the side. The clubhouse is very attractive but small. It has a welcoming look to it. At first it is a little confusing as alongside the putting green is another green which looks like the final hole. But where is it approached from? The course is not immediately apparent as it is over the other side of the road and the second shot into the final green, as at Ganton, has to be played across the road. The 9th fairway can be seen but little else in the way of a golf course is visible beyond a large expanse of field.

Everything about Royal Worlington is understated. Even when you have collected together your clubs and walked across the road to the first tee it is not easy to find. There is no obvious location for it but it is the first tee which you come to. The first hole is a long Par 5 and again it is not absolutely clear in what direction to aim. The hole follows the line of the road and the amount of space is fairly generous though as the hole is flat, there is little perspective until you start walking after your tee shot. In truth it is not a great hole though the designer Harry Colt would approve, as it is a gentle introduction to a round allowing the player to warm up. It does not demand enormous accuracy, nor any particularly demanding shots, to get to the green in three. But if there is a clue to the quality that is to follow, it is in the green which is both enormous and very good quality with long links-like run-off areas.

If the 1st hole is not that challenging , the 2nd soon puts that right. It is a long Par 3 (a driver for me on the day I played) to a raised green. Your shot needs to be accurate in all respects with much thought required as to which is the best side 'to miss', depending on the pin position. Even for low handicap golfers, playing an iron rather than a driver, this is a testing hole. And so is the next, a relatively short Par 4 of 371 yards with a fairly narrow landing area for a good drive and a tricky second to a deceptive green which is larger than it looks and makes judging the distance and getting close to the pin rather awkward.

It is time to mention another feature of Royal Worlington. The third tee shot plays straight across the 2nd green. I was surprised given the prominence of 'health and safety' notices on golf courses these days that there was no mention of this until I looked at the scorecard and found that a whole page is devoted to 'Course Safety'. This is because, as was often the case on traditional courses, the tees are frequently in close proximity to the greens. Just as you play across the 2nd green from the 3rd tee, so too you play across the 4th green from the 5th tee and the 5th green from the 6th tee. No modern designer would consider these as options but in my view it adds to the charm; you just have to keep your wits about you.

The distinctive Halfway Hut at Ganton

The 4th is another Par 5 where the third shot is very tricky with the green sloping away from you down towards a stream. The 5th is a Par 3, not dissimilar to the second though much shorter, with again the green being raised and two-tiered, therefore requiring an accurate shot. This time there is clearly one side to favour; there is a relatively gentle slope off to the right from where pitching back on is fairly easy, while if you miss and fall down the much steeper bank on the left you will have an extremely difficult pitch. The 6th is a long Par 4 which heads back parallel with the 4th and again the approach to the green is tricky especially for a 460 yard hole. I played it as a Par 5. The 7th is another Par 3 with a 'Redan' style green (it slopes down from front to back), so depending again on the pin position offers a degree of risk and reward. The 8th, another long Par 4 of over 460 yards, has a difficult drive with a heavily bunkered fairway before a downhill second where the green becomes an extension of the fairway. Being downhill it plays shorter though judging where to land it requires a little local knowledge. The final hole is then a short Par 4 with a drive across the dog-leg before the second shot across the road into the green sitting in front of the clubhouse. If you are ambitious with your drive you can be left with a very short pitch, yet a cautious three wood will still only leave you with about an 8 iron to the green. Is it worth the risk with a ditch lurking down the right? Even this relatively short hole has its dilemmas.

I have described every hole on Royal Worlington, not because it is just 9 holes but because it is worth making the point that this is not just a 'little 9 hole course'. There is a sort of assumption that a 9 hole course is not a proper course. It feels smaller, so not full-sized. Nothing could be further from the truth at Royal Worlington; this is a full-sized 9 hole course. It is just over 3,100 yards, which is not long by modern standards for 9 holes but this is with three Par 3s. I have also met people who have not been as impressed with the course as I was. It is true that from the 1st tee the impression is underwhelming. You are standing in what looks like a flattish, large open area with a few flags visible on the various horizons. The look of the course is not immediately apparent and the first hole, as I said, does not do a lot to alter this perception. But I think it is a very good test of golf with every hole after the 1st being interesting.

The turf is tremendously good, the greens, with large run-off areas, extremely well kept and there is a very good mix of hole lengths and types. Even big flat greens like the 3rd are challenging. I think the merits of Royal Worlington are subtle and may take time to recognise but they are definitely there.

There is another interesting 9 hole golf course relatively nearby at Flempton, just north of Bury St Edmunds. Again it is not just a 'small' course, being almost exactly the same length as Royal Worlington, this time with two par 3s and just one par 5. It somehow has a smaller feel about it, is less 'linksy' though there are both interesting and challenging holes and it shares the distinction with Royal Worlington and Ganton of the final shot to the green being over a road, though on this occasion it is the road to the clubhouse.

It is probably a good time to discuss again the issue of pace of play. Royal Worlington is primarily a two-ball course though times are available for three and four ball golf. I played a two ball and we got round in just over an hour and a half despite the course being new to us. The members are probably even quicker. There is much to recommend two-ball golf. The only drawback is if you want to combine your golf with a social group of more than one then you need to play foursomes golf where you play alternate shots and many golfers don't like this as they wish always to play their own ball all the way round. Foursomes is a very different game. It is difficult to get a rhythm going and you have to accept that your partner may put you in some difficult positions. (My regular foursomes partner at my club has put me in some VERY unusual places.) In this respect it can also be good for your game, testing you in unusual circumstances, which, after all, is one of golf's challenges. But it is great fun and, being even quicker than playing a two ball singles, is an excellent means of playing a round in a much shorter time. There is no reason why a foursomes match should take more than two and a half hours. I find it particularly enjoyable in winter when perhaps the attractions of being outside for longer are less apparent. While I wouldn't want to be a member of a two-ball only course, I do think that all clubs should reserve times for two-ball play and clubs with the luxury of more than one course should rotate two-and four-ball play between the two.

If the merits of Royal Worlington as a course take a little time to appreciate this is certainly not the case with the delightful clubhouse which oozes character from the moment you enter it. This is like no other clubhouse I know, certainly in this country. You enter straight into a large lounge area which has the feel of a colonial villa with a wooden floor, a glass conservatory-style roof and wicker chairs and tables. The bar is a hatch from where you can order drinks and food. To your right as you enter is a pleasant dining room and there is a large patio area outside overlooking the practice and 18th greens. The changing rooms, it has to be said, are functional rather than luxurious. There is also much to entertain someone with an interest in the history of the game. Royal Worlington is the headquarters of the Cambridge University Golfing Society and there is a board on the wall recording all the past captains. The first in 1890 was none other than Harry Colt, one of my favourite course designers. Other notable captains were Bernard Darwin, the famous golf writer, and Henry Longhurst whose conversational commentary for the BBC in the 1960s and 1970s has become legendary. Other notable members of the society whose names appear in the clubhouse are the cricketer Ted Dexter and the course designer Donald Steel. Spending time in the clubhouse is a very rewarding experience and proper attention is given to the food which is excellent. But to make the most of the experience you must (provided you are not driving) try the club's famous 'Pink Jug'. This esoteric drink is described on the website as 'lemon, ice and champagne and equal tots of Benedictine, brandy and Pimms No.1'. I'm not sure how this particular mix was invented but it is very much part of Royal Worlington's heritage and as they say has 'traditionally been enjoyed by members and visitors alike at the start or at the end of a round at Royal Worlington'.

Perhaps time then to move on from promoting Pink Jug to the local whisky. The distillery was founded by James Nelstrop with his son Andrew who now runs the business. Other family members are also closely involved. The Nelstrops are a farming family which can trace their ancestry back to the 14th century. Originally from Yorkshire, they built a flour mill near Stockport in Cheshire (which remains one of the few independent flour millers still operating today) while another branch of the family moved to Lincolnshire. It is from this latter branch that today's family originates. James had spent a career in various farming related ventures around the world but relatively late in life had the inspiration to develop whisky distilling in Norfolk. There is plenty of logic to this idea as the two main ingredients, barley and water, are both plentiful in the area. Planning permission was obtained in January 2006, first distillations made in December that same year and the distillery opened to the public in August 2007. It is now very much a visitor attraction with tours and a shop as well as a working distillery and, in recognition of this, a large restaurant was also opened in late 2017.

It is worth saying a few words about planning permission. You would have thought that proposals to invest in renovating old buildings in a rural area in order to start a business which will employ a number of people and attract tourism to the area would be gratefully received by planners. Apparently not, as the Nelstrop's initial proposal was turned down because councillors wanted him to site his 'business' on an industrial estate. It took some extensive lobbying and explanations of how the location is part of the experience to get them to change their minds. The Lakes Distillery had similar problems with their initial application. One of the new distilleries planned for Dartmoor, where we are headed in the next chapter, has also had to overcome local objections. In this case it was the architectural design which included the traditional 'pagoda–style' roof which are a feature of many of the older Scottish distilleries. Of course these features were originally part of the process providing vents for malting kilns. As very few distilleries now malt their own barley in house, it has become no more than a distinctive design feature. Local villagers in the village of Princetown objected that the design was 'too Scottish' and not appropriate in Dartmoor. My view is that it is important that these new ventures are sympathetic to the local environment if they are to become part of that environment. A pagoda-style roof is not really a 'Scottish' feature as such but a distillery one. Whether it looks right on Dartmoor or anywhere else can only be answered by looking at the total context. Will the new building and its design and the employment and tourism it promotes enhance the area?

While neither the site nor the buildings quite compete with those at The Lakes Distillery this is a pleasant and pretty spot. There are walks available down to the neighbouring River Thet where willow trees line the banks in a very traditional Norfolk country scene. The tour around the distillery is quite short and the equipment mainly modern and stainless steel. The process is explained in detail as perhaps, unlike in Scotland, the vast majority of their visitors have probably never visited a whisky distillery. The family were advised in the early years by a distiller from Laphroaig who then trained up the current Chief Distiller who had been a brewer at Greene King, the Bury St Edmunds based brewery.

In the first few years of its existence, it was clear what the St George's proposition was. It was a whisky from England and, being the only one, that gave it enough distinctiveness. Now that they are increasingly being joined by new entrants it will be important that they develop a clear marketing proposition. Being just the first in the new wave of English whiskies will not be enough. They are not a micro-distillery – they are a bit more than that which means they have a degree of scale but not enough to be a low cost operator. They have the whole operation on site including the bottling and I noticed that they bottle for private label brands as well. They produce a variety of whiskies; peated and unpeated, blends and single malts as well as rye and malt blends. Most of the maturation seems to be in ex-bourbon barrels so there is no experimentation with other woods and casks. The branding is also quite disparate with the main malt being 'The English' while special editions are released as 'Chapters' from the 'English Whisky Company'. The 'St George's' branding seems to have been replaced though the

'Chapters' designs still use the St George and the dragon motif.

It is often difficult to be the pioneer. This is an impressive business which has innovated and paved the way for others to follow. It has developed a good visitor experience and the investment in the shop and the new restaurant all make sense. My only thought is that more clarity is required on what type of product they intend to produce. I bought a Chapter 6. It was distilled in October 2013 and bottled in November 2016 so is just a three year old whisky. I'm not sure why, and having drunk it I am still not sure where it sits. It is unpeated and the distiller claims on the back that it has '*fresh grassy notes, along with gentle vanilla. Fruity with hints of lime banana and pear. A gentle waft of marzipan. Nose softens with water and is quite nutty (hazelnuts, cashews and almonds).*' If I am honest, I struggled to recognise much of the above. It is a pleasant whisky but if I were offering it to a friend I think the first thing I would tell them is that it was produced in Norfolk and not in Scotland. The new branding of 'The English' seems to suggest them seeing themselves as the definitive English whisky. I'm not sure whether in a few years' time that will be enough.

Incidentally, those of you who read my first book, *Of Peats and Putts*, may remember that I expressed a preference for light, non-peated whiskies. Well, my preferences seem to be changing. I now increasingly like a slightly peaty one. Why? I don't know, but I do know that my tastes are evolving. I think the same is true of wine. Tastes and fashions change. Chardonnay was all the rage until Sauvignon Blanc came along and took over. Now there is a move away from Sauvignon Blanc to dry Rieslings and other more distinctive offerings. (In fact, I increasingly like Chardonnay again. Yes, when it comes to Pouilly, I have of late been opting for Fuissé rather than Fumé which never used to be the case.) The same fashion changes are true in whisky so brands need to be aware of this. The big brands have their flagship 10 or 12 year old malts but have responded with non-age statement releases where they can target different tastes. St George's (or should I call them 'The English'?) will need to do something similar.

CHAPTER FOUR

Devon

'Golf is a metaphor for all the vicissitudes of human experience which test and form the soul.'

J H Taylor (1871-1963)
Five times winner of The Open Championship

HAVING VISITED THE Lake District, Yorkshire and then East Anglia, the natural area for the fourth and final English chapter was the 'West Country'. But whereabouts in this large and varied area? Dorset has some famous and attractive courses; Parkstone, Broadstone, Ferndown and Isle of Purbeck for example, as well as a well-regarded newer course, Remedy Oak, near Wimborne. Wiltshire and Somerset are beautiful counties though perhaps lacking great golf courses; Bernham and Berrow on the Somerset coast perhaps deserves a mention as an obvious exception. The Cotswold Distillery near Shipston-on-Stour and one in Newport on the Isle of Wight are worthy of a visit but neither offer obvious golfing destinations nearby.

I was keen to look at Cornwall as my son lives there. Here there are some great courses such as St Enodoc, Trevose and Royal West Cornwall with slightly less well known ones at Newquay, Perranporth and Mullion. Many of these Cornish courses were designed by famous architects such as Braid and

Colt. There is whisky now being distilled in Cornwall at Hicks and Healey but it is not really a focused whisky operation being more a cider farm with small scale distilling on the side. I'm sure there will one day be a Cornish whisky; there is Cornish everything else these days in this proud county. As well as their famous pasties, you can now buy Cornish tea, Cornish coffee (roasted rather than grown, I assume), Cornish salt, Cornish cheese (yarg is the most famous) and obviously Cornish beer.

In the end the location was dictated by the presence of new distilleries and here the main action is in neighbouring Devon where two new distilleries are emerging. The Princetown Distillery received planning permission in 2017 for a large site with a visitor centre in Princetown. At 1,400 feet above sea level it will become the highest distillery in the UK, a distinction currently enjoyed by Dalwhinnie. The founders claim that the site mimics the conditions of the Scottish Highlands and is therefore ideal for producing quality malt whiskies. The second was at the eastern end of Dartmoor in the small town of Bovey Tracey where the old abandoned Town Hall in the centre of the town has been converted into a distillery. It is this latter one that I have chosen as at the time of writing it is further advanced having started distilling in 2017.

I was pleased to choose Devon as it also enabled me to include a golf course which is a perfect choice; historic, characterful, quirky and in a very scenic location. This is Westward Ho!, founded in 1864, the oldest golf course in England. (The comma immediately after the exclamation mark looks odd but is surely the correct syntax.) It is, I believe, the only place name in the UK with an exclamation mark; the town's name deriving from a novel by the Victorian author Charles Kingsley. So while the golf course is very old in golfing terms, the town itself is not, as it developed and was only named during the mid-19th century. Nearby Bideford is a much older settlement and is a very pretty small town on the estuary of the river Torridge. Kingsley's novel, *Westward Ho!*, was set in Bideford and became a best seller at the time which encouraged local entrepreneurs who were planning to build a new hotel in nearby Northam to change its name from the originally conceived 'Royal Hotel' to Westward Ho!. (If a place name ends with a punctuation mark, do you add a full stop at the end of a sentence? Discuss.) Kingsley even went along to the official opening. The hotel prompted further development in the area and it became a popular resort which quickly came to be called Westward Ho!. In the early 20th century the hotel reverted to its original name of the 'Royal Hotel'. The village, along with the older villages of Northam and Appledore, is situated at the end of the estuary which at that point is joined with that of the River Taw flowing out of Barnstaple. Its position is very scenic looking north westward out into the Bristol Channel where Lundy Island can be seen in the distance. There is a large expanse of beach though it is not quite as large as those slightly further up the coast at Saunton and Woolacombe, both attractive Devon seaside resorts. Saunton, indeed, also boasts a famous golf club with two great links courses, the West and the East, the latter being the highest rated in the county. Indeed the famous Saunton Sands Hotel can be seen from Westward Ho!, sitting high on the cliff further up the coast; it is only about five miles away as the crow flies but to drive you need to cross both estuaries and drive through Barnstaple which can take a good forty minutes.

At some clubs you arrive and immediately get a sense of greatness. Some of the big prestigious courses have quite grand entrances – I think of Royal County Down or Royal Troon. Sometimes the clubhouse is an imposing or distinctive building; Royal Birkdale or St George's Hill come to mind. Or sometimes, it is the view over the course that immediately makes an impression and whets the appetite – St Andrews or Muirfield for example. This is hardly true at Westward Ho!. You arrive in the car park along a narrow village road and park in front of the clubhouse which architecturally is neither particularly noteworthy nor imposing. You are still some distance from the coast and looking out towards it across a large putting green and practice chipping area. Beyond a fence all you can see is a large, rather flat area with sheep grazing on it. 'Where is the golf course?' you say to yourself. If you then look closely you will see the odd flag interspersed with the sheep and conclude that it is in fact there. It is an attractive scene but hardly a typically golfing one.

The club is in fact called 'Royal North Devon'. It was founded as the North Devon and West of England Golf Club in 1864 and was given 'royal' status by the Prince of Wales (the future Edward VII) in 1867. The club's emblem proudly displays the Prince of Wales' feathers. The course, designed by Old Tom Morris, is played over the common land of Northam Burrows. The club's history is inextricably linked with the story of J H Taylor who with James Braid and Harry Vardon was one of 'The Great Triumvirate' who between them won sixteen of the twenty Open Championships between 1894 and 1914 with Taylor contributing five. He was born in nearby Northam, became a member from an early age, and was instrumental in developing the reputation of the club and the course. He became active in amateur golf circles, founding the British Professional Golfers' Association and the Artisan Golfers' Association. He returned in his later life to live in the village of Northam overlooking the course, becoming President of the club in 1957 and sadly dying in 1963 just a year before the club's centenary.

One of my golfing companions when I last visited Westward Ho! was my cousin whose late father (my uncle) had been a well-known amateur golfer, a past captain of the R&A, and for many years closely involved in the staging of the Open Championship. Golf was central to his life and he was a member of numerous clubs all over the UK and beyond. My cousin had heard a story that his father had attended the centenary dinner of Westward Ho! and had allegedly been somewhat the worse for wear after it (not an uncommon occurrence it has to be said) and was therefore intrigued to visit. To his great amusement (and pride) his father's presence at the Centenary celebrations back in 1964 was confirmed in the clubhouse on a large Honours Board for the Club's Gold Medal which showed that in its Centenary year, 1964, it was won by none other than J G Salvesen with a score of 72. It seems he had had every right to be a little the worse for wear after the ensuing dinner.

The clubhouse is an absolute delight, perhaps my all-time favourite. While the outside is, at best, unremarkable inside it is part club, part museum, part country house with a most relaxed atmosphere. It is crammed with memorabilia with lots of Honours Boards, old pictures, trophies of all shapes and sizes, golf clubs and general golfing trinkets. The hub of the clubhouse is a large square room which acts as both a sitting area and a museum. There is a long line of old clubs leant up against one wall and numerous old pictures with captions. The Honours Boards feature many famous names in the early development of golf: Horace Hutchison, Herbert Fowler and Harold Hilton for example. The adjacent bar and dining areas are spacious. If you are visiting Westward Ho!, you must leave time to explore and take in the history, as well as enjoy the bar and food.

To get to the course you walk down past the putting green and through a gate to the first tee. The first hole is a Par 5 but from the tee it is difficult to see the challenge ahead. In this respect it is not unlike the first hole at Royal Worlington though here it is really only on your third shot that you understand the hole. There is a ditch running diagonally across the fairway short of the green which is in fact the hole's main hazard. I talked in *Of Peats and Putts* about what constitutes a great hole and one aspect was the 'look' of it. This hole has no perspective from the tee so cannot be considered a great hole. Having said that I quite like it as it was my only birdie on my last visit. An uncertain drive followed by a speculative rescue club hit in what looked like the right direction put me just over 100 yards short of the green with the ditch safely in between. From there a solid pitch and an impressive 12 foot putt and I was already singing the praises of Westward Ho!. In truth what followed was that, while the holes got much better, my golf deteriorated. The second hole also has little perspective though there is a gentle right to left dog-leg. The green again has little context though in fact it is trickily slightly raised with the ball easily prone to running off. At this stage the course has almost reached the coastline and there is a bank of shingle protecting the course from the sea. The next holes run parallel to the shore and are probably the best on the course. The next two holes are both Par 4s, each with some character, especially the 4th where you drive blind over a dune with an enormous bunker and the second shot is hit to a sunken green.

Walking off the 4th green you are confronted by a large coloured picture of the local hero, J H Taylor, painted on a wall against a dune. It has a caption reminding us that he was '5 times Open Champion'. It is rather a strange tribute to their famous past member. The 5th is a good Par 3 played uphill. The 6th tee now presents a good view over the coast and the estuary up to Saunton. The 6th is Stroke Index 1 (rated the most difficult hole to Par on the course) and it has an appealing drive down onto a very bumpy fairway. There is a dangerous out-of-bounds to the left so with the ever present wind it is actually quite daunting. After the 8th hole, which is a long Par 3 played across a large reed bed, you climb up to the 9th tee from where you get a good view back over the course.

This area of the course has recently been subject to serious coastal erosion with Storm Eleanor in early 2018 breaching the large shingle bar which protects the course from the sea. Many large boulders were strewn across the course and the 8th tee marker was found on the beach. Threat from erosion is obviously a natural hazard of links courses which by definition are built on land reclaimed from the sea. Royal West Norfolk and the new course at Machrihanish Dunes are other examples where the sea has encroached onto the course and it is likely to be an increasing hazard. The old course at Montrose on the east coast of Scotland has similar problems.

As a result, Royal North Devon, despite problematic

relations with Natural England, have agreed upon a redesign of holes 7, 8 and 9 in order to protect the course from further weather incidents. The changes, being undertaken by Mackenzie Ebert are due to be completed during 2019. They will essentially take the holes slightly further inland. To do this, creating new holes on England's oldest course without making them obviously 'new' will be an interesting challenge.

The 9th is a sweeping dog-leg par 5 which begins what is quite a circuitous route back home to the clubhouse. The remaining holes are all played on very flat land which is often the case on the 'inland' side of links courses. This is perhaps flatter than most and it is why Westward Ho! does not have a top reputation as a golf course today. The 12th and 13th holes in particular are very flat and straight and lacking in character though arguably the presence of sheep (and even some wild horses, not to mention wild hares and dog walkers) add to the experience. But the holes are not necessarily easy; they all change direction so judging the wind is always a factor. 14 is a tough long Par 3 and 16 a shorter, slightly more traditional one. Perhaps the trickiest hole is 17, a long Par 5 where again it is difficult to see where best to play. The green is situated across the road which runs up the centre of the course and, unless you are a very long hitter, you need to land your second short of this and the fairway narrows awkwardly at this point. Having said that, it looks more alarming than it really is which is always a clever design feature. The 18th then plays straight back towards the clubhouse where the green is situated just across a ditch giving added pressure on the final shot to the green.

I am always amused to find out how clubs cater for the

obvious hazards that animals on the course bring with them. I remember at Brora, the local rule simply states that 'Animal droppings may be treated as casual water'. At Westward Ho!, the instructions are rather more earthy saying that *a ball which lies in or touches HEAPED OR LIQUID MANURE* (their capitals not mine) *may be cleaned and dropped within one club length'*.

Westward Ho! is a very traditional links experience. The holes have been largely left as they were in 1864. No modern designer (until the recently enforced changes) has tried to add extra features by altering the design. It is very real and I like it for that. It is not a 'great' course but is a hugely enjoyable place to play golf and enjoy the delightful surroundings.

The journey to Bovey Tracey is under 50 miles but can take nearly an hour and a half, the final 15 miles being across the eastern edge of Dartmoor so it is a pretty and rewarding drive, if not a quick one. Many of the roads within the Dartmoor National Park are narrow and so it is best to take your time and enjoy the scenery. Bovey Tracey is a pleasant small town with a history dating back to the early Norman era. It was renowned for its pottery industry from the mid-18th century until it closed down in the 1950s. The town was also the site of a battle in the Civil War.

The distillery is housed in the old Town Hall in the middle of the town. The Grade 11 listed building has had of late a somewhat chequered history acting at times over the years as town council offices, a civic hall and even a fire station and a cinema. With the council having moved to new premises, the distillery has been located in the existing structure with planning permission being sought to restore and upgrade so that a bistro can be incorporated as part of the business plan.

The business was founded by three locals: Greg Millar, Simon Crow, owner of the nearby Edgemoor Hotel, and Andrew Clough. Greg in particular was a whisky enthusiast who made trips to his ancestral Scotland and decided that Devon with its barley, local maltings, water and climate was an ideal location for making whisky. Greg is also a Francophile and it was he who sourced a second hand alembic cognac still which is the centre of the process and very much the distinctive element of the brand's proposition. The still came from a Master Cognac Distiller near Pons in the Cognac region of France and was transported, refurbished and installed ready for the first distillation in 2017. For whisky expertise they teamed up with Frank McHardy, a well-known industry veteran with a long career as a Master Distiller at both Springbank and Bushmills. Frank is another example of a Scot sharing his expertise globally, being involved in distilleries in Australia and Ireland as well as with Dartmoor.

Rather like The Spirit of Yorkshire, this business's focus is on pure distilling. They get their beer wash from a cask brewery in Princetown – the building simply isn't big enough to incorporate a mash tun and wash backs – so the process in the distillery is the distilling and the transfer into maturation barrels. The distillation process requires three primary distillations before a final distillation takes the spirit to about 70% ABV. It looks very different to the traditional Scottish pot stills, comprising three parts - an onion shaped pot still with a swan neck, a central copper wash warmer (which looks like a small inverted pot still) and a condenser tank, all made with 11-12mm hand beaten copper. It is an impressive and attractive piece of kit which dominates the room. The objective is to get as pure a spirit as possible. I had it explained to me that the bulbous neck of the still creates greater reflux with the heavier alcohols within the vapour dropping back and just the sweeter ones coming through. I tasted some raw spirit and it was certainly remarkably fresh and fruity. The still had previously only been used for some of the top brands of cognac including Remy Martin, Hennessy and Martell and it is even thought that there might be some lingering flavours from this use, rather like what is achieved from maturation in wooden barrels. Again I am not sure whether this is a myth or a reality and I'm not sure it matters. What matters is that considerable expertise and care is being given to the process and the quality of the product it produces. They are currently maturing both in the traditional American bourbon barrels and French oak wine barrels with pre-orders available for the release of both three year old and five year old whisky in 2020 and 2022 respectively.

The brand, Dartmoor Whisky, uses a graphic icon of the head of a Dartmoor pony with a clear label giving the brand a distinctive and fresh look. They also use the tag line *The Spirit of Dartmoor* – as new whiskies appear with a local provenance there is a danger that this rather obvious slogan will be overused. Yet, Dartmoor Whisky, like the Spirit of Yorkshire, has a genuine local provenance proposition; their barley is contract grown at Preston Farm on Dartmoor and the malting is undertaken at Tuckers Maltings in nearby Newton Abbott. This process is also the traditional floor maltings which is now very much the exception to the rule in whisky production. The final product will also be bottled locally using Dartmoor spring water.

DEVON

Dartmoor Whisky's pony head logo

The business was financed by a Kickstarter fundraising as well as receiving funds from the European Agricultural Fund for Rural Development. As with all whisky start-ups, cash is a challenge and so the bar, bistro, visitor centre, tours and events are an important part of the business model. Being located in a popular tourist area has to help and should sustain the business – the success of all three of my other featured English distilleries in attracting a high volume of visitors for tours and tastings suggests that this side of the business should do well. After visiting four English distilleries I am not getting a sense of any distinctive 'English Whisky' characteristics. The English whisky industry is always likely to remain a selection of relatively niche players. It is unlikely that a major multinational spirits business will invest in a scale operation in England as it is Scotch and, as we will see, increasingly Irish whiskey which has the international reputation. But this does not stop these new English businesses being successful and indeed it points to what English whisky companies will have in common. Their differentiation will be their small scale and their ability to focus on product quality and they will need to recognise this. The fact that they are not bound by some of the stricter rules of the Scotch whisky regulations can help them in this respect as long as quality remains their prime objective.

The Lakes, The Spirit of Yorkshire and the Dartmoor Distillery are all new ventures and they all use their location in their name with the latter two offering a genuine 'local provenance' story. Whiskies traditionally use where they are as central to their brand proposition. There is something about this in whisky; it belongs to where it is made. The Scotch Whisky regulations actually require the product to be matured in the country to be called 'Scotch', while malt whiskies have regional designations which lie behind this; e.g. Highland, Lowland, Islay etc. So if the Annan distillery, which is only a few miles from the English border, were to hire a warehouse to mature its spirit a few miles away, it would no longer be Scotch.

Here the contrast with gin is stark because there are no origin name protection regulations. There was a recent controversy when the new V&A museum in Dundee thought it would be a good idea to stock local products in its restaurant and included 'Dundee Gin' only to discover that it was actually contract distilled in Birmingham.

I like this sense of belonging to an area which whisky imbues. I much prefer drinking a whisky when I know the distillery and its surrounding area. Provenance is an important trend in food production generally but with whisky this is something more substantial. Single malts come from one distillery and that distillery is part of its location; its topography, its weather, its local people. So the product is not just a recipe; it is a product of its environment. The Lakes will conjure up images of the beautiful Lake District countryside, the Dartmoor Distillery, with its pony head logo, will leave images of Devon while the Spirit of Yorkshire perhaps sides a little more with the Yorkshire personality or 'spirit'. Golf courses are also part of where they are. There have been stories of plans by rich businessmen to recreate the Old Course at St Andrew's perhaps somewhere in Japan. Quite simply, it would not be possible. Even if you matched the layout exactly, it would never be remotely the same. The turf, the angle to the coastline, the weather conditions, the people who greet you; all these contribute to the experience of a round at St Andrew's and you can't re-create this just as you can't re-create a 10 year old Glenlivet in any other distillery. I think that there is one other sport where location is such a factor and that is cricket. Cricket would be very boring if every pitch were the same and the ball bounced and swung and spun the same everywhere it was played. It is the mystery of different pitches allied often to weather conditions which gives cricket much of its interest. A wicket may be 22 yards long but Lords in England in May is very different from Mumbai in February or Sydney in December. While tennis is played on different surfaces, somehow where those surfaces are makes very little difference.

While locality and provenance will be important, each of the new start-ups recognise the need to pursue other differentiators; The Lakes with different woods for maturing, The Spirit of Yorkshire with its unique distilling process and Dartmoor with its distinctive cognac still. This is perhaps the challenge for the original pioneers at The English Whisky Company. With more distilleries opening in England, it will be interesting to see how the industry as a whole develops and how they each pursue a market niche.

Dartmoor Distillery

This distinctive refurbished cognac still dominates the large top floor room at the Dartmoor Distillery. The copper colours, the local brickwork and the bare stone walls all give a rich, warm effect.

Westward Ho! Clubhouse

This central room next to the bar hosts a myriad of old clubs, photographs and other golfing memorabilia depicting the rich history of Royal North Devon Golf Club. Spending time browsing gives you a strong sense of golfing history.

CHAPTER FIVE

Wales

'Welsh Whisky is the most wonderful Whisky that ever drove the skeleton from the feast, or painted landscapes in the brain of man. It is the mingled souls of peat and barley washed white with the waters of the Tryweryn. In it you will find the sunshine and the shadow which chased itself over the billowy fields, the breath of June, the carol of the lark, the dew of the night, the wealth of summer and autumn's rich content – all golden with imprisoned light. Drink it, and you will hear the voice of men and maidens singing the "Harvest Home", mingled with the laughter of children. Drink it, and you will feel within your blood the startled dawns, the dreamy tawny dusks of perfect days. Drink it, and within your soul will burn the bardic fire of the Cymri, and their law-abiding earnestness. For many years this liquid joy has been within staves of oak, longing to touch the lips of man, nor will its prototype from the Sherry Casks disdain the more dulcet labial entanglement with any New or Old Woman.'

*Advertisement for The Welsh Whisky Distillery
at Frongoch, near Bala (circa 1890)*

It seems a pity that the Advertising Standards Authority would not allow such an advertisement today. I can understand the need for restrictions on the advertising of alcohol but there are many walks of life where humour is now a victim of legislation.

Sadly this distillery closed after only a few years of operation and there was a gap of over one hundred years before whisky was again produced in Wales. At time of writing, there are three whisky distilleries. 2018 saw the opening of the Aber Falls Distillery in Gwynedd in North Wales. This is a new enterprise set up by Halewood International, a large independent spirits business which has developed a wide portfolio of new gins and now sees premium malt whisky as another market opportunity. In the south west, the Da Mhile is an artisan distillery which has been producing organic gin and spirits since 2012 and has subsequently started to distil whiskies too. But the most famous Welsh whisky is Penderyn which was the first new distillery to be opened outside Scotland in the UK, pre-dating both the English Whisky Company by some two years and the revival of the industry in Ireland. Situated in the village of Penderyn on the southern tip of the Brecon Beacons it certainly fits my criteria on location and setting.

The south Wales coastline is rich in great golf courses. The best is unarguably Royal Porthcawl, a magnificent course which has held many major amateur tournaments as well the British Seniors Open. It also has a marvellous clubhouse which is full of character with its distinctive red roof and delightful views out to sea. But there are others; next door to Porthcawl, Pyle and Kenfig is a charming links course though slightly inland. The back 9 is, in my view, vastly superior to the front 9 but it is worth playing. In addition there is Southerdown, Ashburnham and, further along the coast, Tenby. Of course, I haven't mentioned Celtic Manor, the location for the 2010 Ryder Cup; let's just leave it at that. My choice, however, is Pennard, which happens to be geographically the most proximate to Penderyn though this was not the reason why. It wins handsomely on all of my criteria; it is not the most famous in the area yet has a proud history, it is stunningly scenic situated on the Gower Peninsula overlooking Three Cliffs Bay, and it is a thoroughly delightful test of golf (as long as you approach it with the right attitude – I will explain later).

Harry Vardon

Let us start at Penderyn. The village is best approached from the north. Crossing the Severn into Wales, while it is a longer route, it is worth heading north to join the A40 at Abergavenny and head north-west along it through the delightful town of Crickhowell and onto Brecon where you turn left and drive down through the National Park into Penderyn. The scenery is spectacular with the road after Brecon climbing high into the Beacons before you drive down into Penderyn.

It is claimed that archaeologists have found evidence of stills in Wales as early as the 4th Century. This may be an attempt by

Wales to claim bragging rights for discovering whisky before the Scots and the Irish. There is clearer evidence of a distillery in Dale in Pembrokeshire in the early 18th century owned by the Williams family. It was a member of this family, Evan Williams, who then emigrated to America and founded Kentucky's first distillery in 1783. Evan Williams is now a well-known brand of straight bourbon owned by the privately owned Heaven Hill Company. There seems to have been little activity in Wales then until the 1880s when, with distilleries across Scotland and Ireland booming, the Welsh Whisky Company (the one with the humorous advertising agency) opened at Frongoch near Bala in North Wales. Unfortunately, as aforementioned, it had a very short-lived history closing in 1903. It was then nearly one hundred years later that Penderyn started distilling with its first malt being launched on St David's Day in 2004.

I talked earlier about both The Spirit of Yorkshire and the Dartmoor Distillery innovating by focusing on distilling and manufacturing their mash at a local brewery. In fact it was Penderyn which first took this approach working with Brains Brewery. Penderyn also innovated with their still, designing a process around the use of a unique single pot still designed by Sir David Faraday, a descendant of the famous scientist, Michael Faraday. The still's main feature is the copper column (which is split into two in order to fit into the building) with a series of plates through which the vapour passes, each one refining the product further. Spirit is drawn off at the seventh plate with other vapours refluxed back into the first column. So is this 'single distilled' or is it 'multiple distilled in a single process'? To this amateur, it seems similar to what the Spirit of Yorkshire is doing with its column attached to the conventional pot stills. In this respect it is no surprise to find that Penderyn also worked with Dr Jim Swan who was instrumental in the set-up in Yorkshire.

As the first new distillery in the UK outside Scotland, Penderyn was an almost immediate success. It is interesting when talking to friends about writing this second book, they all question '*Are there any whisky distilleries in England?*', yet most had heard of Penderyn. This success, which included a strong export business in France and Germany, required an increase in capacity and a second 'Faraday still' was installed in 2013, but interestingly they also have purchased two traditional Scottish-style pot stills in order to enable them to broaden the range of whisky types they can produce. They have also now brought their mash process in-house and have a mash tun and wash backs as you would expect in a conventional malt distillery. The growth in capacity has meant that any original thoughts about only using Welsh barley have been put to one side - the majority now comes from England. Indeed the sales success led to an announcement in late 2018 that Penderyn was opening a second distillery in Swansea at the old Swansea Copperworks. As copper is an important part of a pot still distillery it seems an appropriate site. Swansea Council, with a National Lottery grant, has plans to redevelop the area and Penderyn is to be a central part of it by restoring the old Powerhouse. As well as the distillery, there will be a visitor centre - the area is close to the famous football and rugby Liberty Stadium so the opportunity for greater visitor numbers is obvious.

Penderyn was also somewhat ahead of the trend on maturation. None of its products include age statements, something which has become commonplace across the industry but at the time was the exception to the rule with premium malts. Their main approach was to mature in ex-bourbon casks with finishing in Portuguese Madeira barriques. Sherry, port and premium wine barrels are also used to finish for particular expressions. They never planned to produce peated whiskies but now produce a product that is finished in ex-Laphroaig casks which gives it a subtle peated taste. The marketing of the different product types is unashamedly 'Welsh' with their core 'Dragon' range and their special edition 'Icons of Wales' range which includes a Bryn Terfyl, a Dylan Thomas and even 'That Try', commemorating the famous Gareth Edwards try for the Barbarians against the All Blacks in 1973.

Their marketing is strong and active. They have recently invested in a new bottle design with a very distinctive shape. Actually I am not sure it was necessary as I quite liked the simplicity of their original bottle. There is also a touch of humour in the design as each bottle carries the letters 'AC', which in this case don't stand for 'appellation contrôlée' but 'Aur Cymru', or, in English, 'Welsh Gold' which is represented on the design by a gold seam device. The distillery now has a very professional visitor centre with a small museum and a shop and being in a popular tourist area has meant that they attract over 40,000 visitors a year. As well as the standard tours explaining the history and the process, they hold masterclasses and I was particularly attracted by a Whisky and Chocolate tour in conjunction with a local handmade chocolate business in Pontypridd.

The whole issue of whisky and food pairing is increasingly popular in the same way as it has always been with wine. Again much depends on the occasion but I sometimes like to accompany a meal with whisky rather than wine. I generally add a little more water than usual and, while I've never thought much about it, I can see that seafood, for example, will be better with a lighter, ex-bourbon cask whisky while a heavy beef stew may need something more flavoursome such as a sherry or port finish. I still prefer to drink whisky at the end of the meal and here I make the case for whisky to accompany desserts, cheese and chocolate. In my view, whisky complements each of these better than most wines. I've heard it said that the problem with cheese is that you need a different whisky with each cheese you try which makes things a little expensive. I am particularly partial to a post-prandial whisky with some strong dark chocolate and I have found that all good malts go well with that. As to whisky and chocolate, I think it could be an important subject for a detailed study and I would certainly volunteer to be involved.

The site of the new distillery in Swansea will be only about ten miles from Pennard. It is, however, just under an hour's drive from Penderyn itself down the valley of the River Neath to Neath itself, through Swansea and onto the Gower peninsula. The club's history is a bit sketchy. The land on which the course was built is the Pennard Burrows which were part of the Kilvrough Estate owned by the Penrice family. In 1896 Thomas Penrice entered into an arrangement which enabled a small club, restricted to just twenty members, to play golf over the land. When he died, his daughter inherited the estate and in 1908 the club was reconstituted with a less restrictive lease and began to develop. At some stage (it's not clear when) James Braid was hired to develop the layout which has not changed substantially since, though Ken Cotton and Donald Steel are both credited with some upgrades.

The course is a delight, but I warn golfers who may still worry that links style golf is a little too uncertain for their liking that they should stay away. Every hole has interest and challenge some of which will be frustrating and border on the ridiculous, hence the need to approach it with the right attitude. It cannot be described as a 'fair' course as much (perhaps much more than on an average links course) will depend on the luck of the bounce. There are many blind and semi-blind shots so it is a course which, to fully appreciate it, you need to play more than once. But it will always test the mind, the spirit and the soul and thus delivers exactly what a good golf course should. I am sure that members will never tire of playing here as every round will be different - so often not true of more humdrum courses. This isn't just a typical old links. It is links golf in the extreme; it is 'links max' and all the more fun as a result.

I referred earlier to George Waters' book *Sand and Golf* which makes the case for sandy soil being the key to proper golf. There is also a wonderful website called *Fine Golf* which basically defines proper golf as the ability to play what it describes as *'the running game'*. So whether it is true links or sandy soil or classic heathland, the key factor is that the ball runs as opposed to plugs in the ground. The website is actually quite technical in discussing soil and grass types and greenkeeping methods which are suitable for this type of golf and maintains that the use of the right grasses is critical. It is certainly an education and has opened my mind to a much broader understanding of what delivers a great golf course. I also like the website's author's maxim that a round of golf should deliver that *'joy to be alive'* feeling. This attunes to my view that golf is not just the game, the sport; it is much more than that, involving the company and the environment in which it is played with the look and feel of the course playing a central role in the latter. And a good look and feel does not mean a manicured look; indeed often quite the contrary. It should be a natural look in tune with its environment. Pennard is an excellent example of this. And the day I played, it was one of those perfect days. There was bright sunshine and a cloudless sky. There was a pleasant seaside breeze. The views were spectacular. The company was familiar and convivial. It felt '*a joy to be alive*'.

On that day the quality of my golf did not quite deliver but it didn't matter. In most rounds there are good shots to remember and what makes the difference is how many bad shots you play. Often all I need is for there to be one great shot in a round, a shot I can not only savour at the time but remember afterwards. Rounds of golf are like that; made up of good things and not so good things and occasionally a shot where you really hit the sweet spot and the ball does exactly what you wanted it to. Again non-golfers may not appreciate the delight which this gives. It is rather like listening to music; a round of golf is like a symphony with a structure and themes. Some rounds are better than others just as with musical works. Some are great and others not so great. And even in average rounds there can be moments of excellence, moments which transcend the normal. I find this in music; tiny moments in symphonies, maybe just a few notes, which achieve something special and are generally fleeting but which you remember and hold onto and which you yearn to experience again. I find this with Mendelssohn, perhaps not the greatest composer but a composer of great moments of music; you could perhaps say the same of Freddie Mercury and Queen. As golfers we can all create great moments of golf but a full 18 holes' of greatness – a completely sublime symphony of golf – is very rare.

I think that this must also apply to whiskies though I am not enough of a connoisseur to judge. There is an enormous and growing market for premium expressions from famous distilleries. It is the job of the master blender to create these. He or she has to judge what stock to use; what age of whisky and what mix of, for example, bourbon and/or sherry barrel-matured whisky. Is there a role for a special wine or port barrel finish? The options are endless but creating that perfect expression can be elusive. The master blender is like a composer of a symphony seeking to create perfection – there may be barrels of great whisky but how do you combine them to create something special? A great symphony has themes which come together and the whole becomes greater than the sum of its parts. That is what a master blender is also striving to achieve.

The front 9 is the more inland of the two with two good Par 3s at 2 and 5 which is sharply downhill to a well-protected green. A number of other holes are worth a mention: 3 is a dog-leg par of less than 400 yards but proves that a good par 4 does not have to be long, especially as it is likely to be into the prevailing wind; 7 is called 'Castle' and heads out towards the ruin of Pennard Castle which is perched up on the highest point overlooking the bay. The 8th plays back as a dog-leg with a narrow fairway and a tricky second shot to a small elevated green. 9 is then a straight drive to a 90 degree dog-leg from where the second shot has to be accurate to hit the green which is perched on a dune.

If anything the back 9 has even more character. 10 is an

extreme Par 5; a sharply downhill drive to an almost 90 degree dog-leg and then sharply uphill and into the prevailing wind to the green. 11 is an intimidating Par 3 across a valley to a green in a hillside dune with not many good places to miss it. 13 is another tough par 3 of over 200 yards before 14 plays back as another dog-leg, not unlike the 8th. Whether or not you are playing off the back tee, it is worth walking back and up to it as it is the highest point on the course and affords a magnificent view of Three Cliffs Bay, the coastline and the course. 16 and 17 are both distinctive Par 5s with your drive needing to favour the right on the former and the left on the latter. Between playing them, again take a little time to enjoy the magnificent views from around the 16th green and 17th tee.

It is probably not a course for the purist, even a links or 'running golf' purist. The course's look is distinctly 'unmanicured' though I like that as it feels very natural. In this respect it reminds me of Brora and indeed in both places cattle still have roaming rights which can lead to this natural look. The variety of holes and the variety of shot types required make it, in my view, a great golf course, one which is both intellectually stimulating and emotionally rewarding.

For a traditional club it is quite modern in outlook and markets itself with the tagline 'The Links in the Sky'. This is a clever description as while it neighbours the sea it is from a considerable height, more like a clifftop than a true links. But the style is unashamedly 'linksy' (in fact extremely 'linksy') and I will no longer discuss whether it is truly a links as it definitely has sandy soil and delivers 'the running game' which I have learned is the key factor. The clubhouse is modern and practical and the operation was on my visit efficiently managed by a lady Secretary – I mention this as it remains the exception rather than the rule for golf clubs. The membership is very diverse and in this respect reminds me of the best of the small Scottish clubs. It represents the community it serves. It sees itself as more than just a golf club offering a range of flexible membership options as well as opening its restaurant to the public and encouraging walkers to enjoy what it offers.

The Pro-shop is welcoming and well stocked. Most club professionals nowadays understand the need to market themselves. Some of the very old traditional clubs did not have shops. Muirfield does not have one to this day. I remember arriving at Western Gailes on the Ayrshire coast in the late 1990s and one of our group asked for the Pro-shop and was told that if he needed some tees or balls, they were available from the bar. Nowadays most clubs have shops with a wide array of merchandise from clubs and clothes to drinks and snacks to sustain the golfer over 18 holes. I always like to buy a memento of a visit to a new golf club. A friend of mine always buys a ball with the club logo on it and he has a wall in his study with now hundreds of balls. Another friend often buys a jersey with a logo but depending on how many golf courses you visit there are only so many golf jerseys you need. Last time I went to Brora I bought socks with the new club logo embroidered on them. I am a bit mean and generally buy the cheapest item which is usually a ball marker. These have the advantage of you being able to use them rather than just collect them. Mind you ball markers come in all shapes and sizes these days. Again, I am a traditionalist and I dislike some of the larger ones. There has been a trend to make them like gambling chips; large, thick and garish. I dislike these for many reasons not least because they can be impractical when the idea of marking a ball on the green is often as a courtesy to your playing partner, so the less visible the better. The ones I like the best are the very small ones with a small stem to anchor them on the green. Most nowadays are coin-like and again I don't like these if they are too thick or have a convex top. Yes, I am fussy but there you are. The marketers like bigger ones to show off the club logos but I think there is much to be said for small and discreet. While I am on the subject, I am also fussy about tees. I much prefer wooden ones. Yes, they break but I like to have a handful in my pocket, some long and some short for irons at Par 3s. I can understand the logic of why people use the large plastic ones which you insert into the ground and give a consistent height. But they look ugly and unsightly and are very often garishly coloured. And I am not so sure that having precisely the same height of tee every time is that important – there are surely many more variables in the average swing. Finally, I think there is an environmental case for wooden tees but maybe that is stretching the argument. I can see that I am going to run out of potential playing partners now that I have outlawed large ball markers and plastic tees.

The same is true in whisky distillery shops. The best memento to buy is clearly a bottle which is what I usually do. Some shops will then have other branded merchandise; keyrings, scarfs, pencils. I'm not a fan as they have nothing to do with whisky. My only other item which I like to buy is a whisky glass. This is a whole subject in itself. Many people, when thinking of a whisky glass or a whisky tumbler, envisage a round, upright crystal glass. Of course, this is not the right shape of glass to use for a malt whisky. You need a shape where you can gently swirl the whisky and 'nose' it. The glass should be tactile as it is very much part of the drinking experience. There are a number of different whisky glasses which I do like and if I see a new shape I buy one with the result that I now have a selection of about ten. There is the traditional 'Glencairn' shape which looks a bit like a pot still with an open top. These can come in different sizes. There are then broader ones with more open tops but still a wider base to allow the 'swirl'. The English Whisky Company had a glass with a stem which looks more like a sherry glass. One of my favourites (though it is a bit of a gimmick) is the round bottomed glass I bought at Bunnahabhain. Yes, it does not have a flat base but is cleverly designed just to wobble rather than fall over and spill – a metaphor perhaps for the after effects of enjoying a good dram. So when I approach my whisky cabinet of an evening I have two choices to make: which whisky will it be and in which glass shall I drink it? These are the sort of dilemmas that I can cope with in life.

It is difficult to identify any specific 'Welshness' about either Wales' golf courses or its whisky. With its magnificent coastline, it is not surprising that Wales can boast a number of great courses. Penderyn is an unashamedly Welsh business but, being a pioneer in starting a whisky distillery outside of Scotland and Ireland, would merit inclusion in any review of the industry wherever it were situated. I see Penderyn producing innovative and distinctive products and not relying on its Welsh heritage for its differentiation.

CHAPTER SIX

Leinster

'Usquebaugh: An Irish or Erse word, which signifies the water of life. It is a compounded distilled spirit, being drawn on aromaticks; and the Irish sort is particularly distinguished for its pleasant and mild flavour. The Highland sort is somewhat hotter; and, by corruption, in Scottish they call it whisky.'

Samuel Johnson (1709-1784)
A Dictionary of the English Language

I LOVE FERRY trips - readers may remember the ones to Campbeltown and on to Islay which I described in *Of Peats and Putts* - so it is tempting to travel from Wales to neighbouring Ireland in this manner. From Pennard it is a couple of hours to Fishguard where ferries sail to Rosslare in the south east of Ireland. Alternatively it is about four hours to Holyhead on Anglesey (on the way you could take in two of Wales' other great courses, Aberdovey and Royal St David's at Harlech) where the ferries sail to Dublin, but somehow these ferry journeys do not hold the same charms – it is sea and just sea most of the way without any of the delightful scenery of the western Scottish Isles and the southern Hebrides. So maybe a flight is both quicker and easier.

In Ireland I wanted both a geographical spread and a mix of distillery type. At the turn of the century it would not have been possible to feature four Irish distilleries as there were only three remaining: Middleton, Cooley and Bushmills. This was a sad state of affairs for an industry which a hundred years previously had matched that of Scotland in its size and influence. I will discuss a brief history of the Irish whiskey industry later but there has been a dramatic renaissance in the past ten years with numerous new openings and significant new investments from both the big multi-national players and local entrepreneurs. Irish whiskey is the fastest growing segment of the world whisky market. I have therefore chosen a range of types; one old established player, though now internationally owned, one new multinational investor and two entrepreneurial start-ups. And I have taken one from four geographically disparate regions. Originally I had thought that these could be from each of the four traditional Provinces of Ireland: Leinster, Ulster, Connaught and Munster, now mainly known as rugby teams. However, I wanted to include Donegal (for reasons which you will learn) and discovered, of course, that Donegal was part of the original 'Ulster', being one of three Ulster counties that voted in a referendum to go with the Irish Free Sate at the time of Irish Independence in 1922.

I am starting in Leinster which is the province which includes Dublin. Unsurprisingly, this has probably the biggest choice of both courses and distilleries. Starting with golf, there are numerous world renowned courses within easy reach of Dublin, from the K Club which hosted the Ryder Cup in 2006, to Mount Juliet and Druids Glen. The most famous traditional course is Portmarnock, a 27-hole links just north of the city, while Royal Dublin, nearer the centre of the city, is the oldest. There is also a magnificent new links called The European Club at Brittas Bay in County Wicklow about an hour to the south. This was created some thirty years ago by Pat Ruddy, a famous Irish course designer, who we will come across elsewhere, particularly in our visit to Donegal. Ruddy came from a modest background in County Sligo and was a successful amateur golfer but golf course design became his passion. His dream was to build his own course and this was realised in the late 1980s with The European Club. It also enhanced his reputation and is why his name is attached to many subsequent upgrades of the major links of Ireland. The Irish love their golf so it is not surprising that there are so many great courses in easy reach of the capital. My choice, however, is perhaps the least well known, though it is in fact only 20 minutes' drive from Dublin Airport situated on a peninsula overlooking the northern Dublin commuter town of Malahide.

The Island Golf Club was established in 1890 so is one of the oldest courses in Ireland, predating its more famous near neighbour, Portmarnock, by some four years. One of the reasons for it being less famous is that for about the first 80 years of its existence it was only reachable by boat from Malahide. It was not until the 1970s that a road was built and it was at this time that significant changes were made to the course. The story of the founding of The Island is interesting. A number of members of Royal Dublin, which had been founded a few years earlier, were frustrated at not being allowed there to play on Sundays and decided to look for other options. Four of them rowed across from Malahide to survey the land and decided it would make a good golf course. A lease was agreed with the local landowner and the ten friends formed 'the Syndicate' becoming the founder members of the club. They only allowed other members (men from 1896 and ladies a year later) to join as 'annual ticket holders' so that they retained control. This syndicate was something of a closed shop with new ones appointed as others passed on and the club was run in this way until the 1950s when they sold their interest to the existing 'annual ticket holders'. A significant upgrade to the course was undertaken by Fred Hawtree in the 1970s making it the great course it is today.

I last played The Island on a late afternoon in April, teeing off within an hour of landing at Dublin airport. While it is only a short drive, the last few miles are very tortuous and the road is not wide. We were given a very friendly welcome and, as it was late in the day, an unofficial 'twilight' rate was offered as the course was also not busy. We had just over three hours of decent light left but, playing as a two ball on an empty course, that was ample.

There is something magical about evening golf. I definitely prefer playing golf late in the day rather than early. There is something about evening light which lends itself to golf and while I also enjoy early morning walks, it is not my preferred time for playing golf. I know a lot of people who like to play golf early and finish by mid-morning so that they can either get back to their families or still have time for some other endeavour. I prefer the other way round. Golf is a contemplative game and it is somehow easier to do this late in the day. While, as you will have gathered, I like to play golf at a good pace, the evening atmosphere with the lengthening shadows gives the impression that time slows down. It can be a very special feeling.

Good evening light, of course, requires decent weather and we were lucky. It was late April and there were clouds about, so the sun was intermittent, but it was dry and bright. There was a good breeze which to me is a prerequisite of a good round of links golf. Links golf without a breeze seems wrong; on those rare windless seaside days it feels as if something is missing. It is chocolate cake without the icing. Yet while there was a breeze, there was also a stillness and a gentleness to the surroundings. This is not a coastal landscape with crashing waves but an estuary setting with birds and other wildlife. The views are not spectacular but they are rewarding and comforting.

The Island, being built on a peninsula, has sea on three sides with enormous dunes so the scenery is arresting in every direction. When the course was redesigned in the 1970s, the clubhouse was moved from the landing stage opposite Malahide further up the inland side of the peninsula. It is a delightful piece of land, largely unspoilt and home to a rich array of fauna and flora. The front 9 starts by heading across from the west to the eastern side before heading up the peninsula. All the holes require thought, wending their way amidst high dunes. The back 9 is perhaps the more noteworthy. The 10th is a long par 5 playing due south and hugging the estuary. 11 heads back north and 12 (aptly named 'Valhalla') has a tricky second shot over a valley to a raised green. 13 is a lovely Par 3, a tough hole at the tip of the peninsula with Malahide as the back drop. The land is a little flatter at the tip but as you head back you enter the vast expanse of duneland. The 14th on the eastern side has what must be the narrowest fairway in links golf and as such offers a somewhat scary drive with a lateral water hazard all the way up the right hand side. The 15th is a Par 5 with a green lying below an enormous bank of high dunes. 16 plays back southwards uphill to a raised green and 17 heads further up the eastern coastline before 18 takes you back across to the clubhouse on the western side. As you will see from this, every direction is catered for so whatever the wind direction of the day you will have every type of shot tested.

The clubhouse is modern but very friendly and when I last lunched there the food was excellent and the service exceptionally friendly and attentive. The Island has come of age and has been a regional qualifying venue for The Open for a number of years and in 2019 it will co-host The Amateur Championship with Portmarnock. With The Open returning to Royal Portrush in the same year, 2019 will be a landmark year for Irish golf.

Before embarking on our tour of Irish distilleries it is worth covering a brief history. The development of the industry has been heavily influenced by politics, even more so than in Scotland, because of the Home Rule and independence struggles. There is some evidence of distilling as early as the 12th century though it is more likely to have developed during the 16th century when grain cultivation became widespread. Taxing both producers and inns became part of the English Crown's attempt to impose rule on Ireland. As in Scotland, before the Excise Act of 1823 much of the industry was illegal distilling of 'poteen' with 'legal' whisky being heavily taxed and dismissed as 'Parliament whisky' with the knowledge that the taxes were being used to finance an English army, thereby breeding understandable resentment. So the level of taxation and the resentment it caused fuelled demand for 'illegal' poteen. The more the government tried to control distilling through taxation and licensing the more they incentivised illicit production. Eventually this was recognised (Adam Smith's famous works discussing the power of incentives were published in the second half of the 18th century) and the 1823 Excise Act reduced the level of duty thereby making legal distilling more profitable and reducing the incentives for making poteen. The development of Midleton, the biggest distillery in Ireland today, dates from this time as well as the other famous names of the Irish industry; Jameson, Power and Roe, all Dublin companies which built distilling businesses. From 1825 to 1870 production doubled and then doubled again by the turn of the century, despite the many social and political challenges, not least the dreadful famine of the 1840s which reduced the country's population through death and emigration by over two million. Much of the success was export led so by 1900 there were some 30 distilleries producing nearly 40 million litres of spirit.

The 20th century, by contrast, proved to be a dire time for the Irish whiskey industry with most of the damage done in the first two decades. The boom of the 1890s had led to over-production and this, combined with an economic downturn in the UK and Europe in the first decade of the new century, sent prices crashing. This was then followed by the Great War which further damaged markets while the UK government, worried about the effects of alcohol consumption on the war effort, both increased taxes on spirits and established the Control Board (Liquor Traffic) in 1915 which imposed restrictions on alcohol sales and consumption. Soon the use of barley was forbidden for anything but food production effectively ending whisky production from barley upon which the Irish industry relied. To make things worse, immediately after the war in 1920, the United States, Irish whiskey's other main export market, introduced Prohibition which lasted until 1933 by which time the industry had almost collapsed. Amidst all this, the fight for Irish Independence, which had been re-ignited with the 1916 Easter Rising, gave an unhelpfully unstable political backdrop to any attempts to revive the industry. Exports to England and the British Empire were hampered by trade disputes which followed independence while a law passed by the new Irish state, intended to protect Irish whiskey's premium image by requiring Irish whiskey to have matured for five years rather than three, had the unintended consequence of reducing the level of stocks available for export once Prohibition had ended in the US.

It is interesting to compare the fortunes over this period with those of the Scottish industry which was faced with many of the same circumstances, political independence apart, but suffered less badly. Much of this was a result of the slightly different routes which the respective industries had taken during the 19th century with Scotland embracing the patent still process and blending to a much greater extent than Ireland and thus becoming a lower cost producer and not reliant on barley. I will explain later in the book the differences between the new patent stills and the traditional pot stills. Yet it could have been so different; it is surprising to learn that in the 1860s more Irish whiskey was sold in Scotland than Scotch whisky. Indeed, Irish pot still whiskey and Cognac rather than Scotch were considered the sophisticated drinks in society circles in late Victorian times. Scotch was only later to benefit from the misfortunes of these two market leaders; the phlloxera epidemic wiping out cognac production and the political turmoils of Ireland hampering Irish whiskey's growth prospects. The differences between Scotch and Irish Whiskey, both historically and now, is something I will explore further as I tour Ireland.

Whisky Barrels

While the Scottish industry began its revival before the Second World War it was not until the 1950s that there were signs of life in Ireland. Production in mid-century was probably no more than a tenth of the level of 1900 and the government had worsened matters by continually increasing tax rates which only put further pressure on volumes. In 1950 legal definitions for Irish Whiskey and Irish Pot Still Whiskey were established requiring the product to be distilled from barley and matured in Ireland, the latter only in copper pot stills and with a mix of malted and unmalted barley. Later the minimum maturation time allowed was reduced from five years to three while the government even helped fund advertising campaigns for export sales during the 1960s which brands like Tullamore

Dew took advantage of. Meanwhile the industry had begun to adopt the patent still and blending and introduce a wider range of products. In the mid-1960s the few remaining firms in the Republic of Ireland merged to form United Distillers of Ireland with brands like John Jameson & Sons, Cork Distillers and John Power & Son falling under the same owner. This led to the investment in a new low-cost distillery at Midleton, near Cork, which produced all the brands as different blends from a patent still process. Jameson gradually became the lead brand, especially for export, and began to have significant success worldwide. It was this which attracted Pernod Ricard, the French multinational spirits business, to buy the company in 1988 to add to its growing portfolio and sales have gone from strength to strength since. So by the end of the century, while there were only three remaining distilleries (Midleton, Cooley, a new distillery opened in 1989, and Bushmills, where we will visit in the next chapter), the industry had begun a revival and the platform had been put in place for the explosion of new distilleries, products and brands which we have seen over the past ten years.

Today distilling is returning to Dublin for the first time since Irish Distillers closed down its Dublin plants in the 1970s. In the 19th century there were believed to be thirty seven. Recently four new enterprises have been started in the famous Liberties area of the city. First, two brothers from the Teeling family opened a distillery in 2015. Their father, John Teeling, had created the first new distillery in Ireland in the 20th century when it opened Cooley in 1989, building the business successfully before selling it, as well as Kilbeggan, which he had revived some years later, in 2011 to Beam Inc.

(subsequently to become Beam Suntory). Bacardi now has a minority stake in this new enterprise, its first involvement in the whiskey industry. Then Pearse Lyons opened in 2017. Dr Pearse Lyons, who died in 2018, had worked for Irish Distillers before emigrating to America, founding an animal feeds company and also opening a distillery in Kentucky in 2008. He then, through a joint venture, opened a distillery back in his native Ireland in Carlow. The stills from Carlow have now been moved back to Dublin where the famous St James's Church has been converted into a distillery. In 2018, The Dublin Liberties Distillery, owned by a UK spirits business, installed three stills in an old converted mill near St Patrick's Cathedral. Finally Diageo, having surprisingly exited the Irish industry by selling Bushmills (more to follow in the next chapter) has decided it is losing out on the action and is reviving the Roe & Co brand, one of the historic Dublin distilling companies which owned the largest distillery in the country, and is building a distillery in the old Power House of its Guinness site at St James Gate. All these investments are accompanied by smart visitor centres which will take advantage of Dublin's increasing popularity as a tourist destination. This very much mirrors what is happening in Edinburgh; until recently the capital of Scotland had no distilleries and just a few whisky shops as well as The Scotch Whisky Experience visitor attraction on The Royal Mile. Now, three distilleries are due to open in the capital, all with big visitor centres including Diageo's plans for a home for its world leading brand, Johnnie Walker.

In summary, a huge opportunity to utilise Ireland's whiskey heritage to leverage the current market growth has been recognised and this is being exploited by both local entrepreneurs and multinational spirits organisations, especially those with American roots. We will see this everywhere we go in Ireland.

I have chosen a new distillery outside Dublin situated on the River Boyne in County Meath about 40 minutes north of the city. Here lies Slane Castle, an old Irish estate owned by the Conyngham family. The castle dates from the early 18th century and boasts gardens designed by Capability Brown. The castle was probably best known in Ireland as a venue for numerous rock concerts which have featured a distinguished set of names: U2, Bob Dylan, Guns'n Roses, The Rolling Stones, Bruce Springsteen, David Bowie, Queen and REM. These started back in the 1980s with Slane Castle subsequently becoming a world renowned venue as the family looked for ways to fund a major renovation programme after a disastrous fire in 1991 caused devastating damage to the castle.

The family were always looking for enterprises to fund the costs of maintaining the estate and founded a whisky brand some years ago, the product being produced at Cooleys. Then in 2015 a €50m investment was announced to convert the stable block into a new distillery. €50m? Where was that coming from? The answer was simple: Jack Daniels, or rather Brown Forman, the owner of the Jack Daniels brand, the world's largest whiskey (whiskey, not whisky) brand. Brown Forman also owns Southern Comfort and Woodford Reserve. It is the same story; Irish whiskey has powerful heritage which international, particularly American, multinational companies want to exploit. Having an Irish whiskey as part of its international portfolio is seen as a big opportunity.

You can see where the money has been spent. The old stable block was architecturally impressive (it was also designed by

Capability Brown, his only building design in Ireland) but had been in a poor state of repair and the buildings have been sensitively restored to respect the original design. Particularly impressive is the restoration of the enormous cobbled courtyard while the old stable block has been converted into a café and bar. The distillery comprises three copper pot stills and six column stills and wooden washbacks. The visitor centre is impressive providing tours which both cover the family and local history as well as explaining the distilling process. There is a well-stocked shop and a bar area where you can enjoy a dram in your own stable stall. The guide when I visited was a local resident but had clearly had professional training and was dressed in an expensive uniform. Certainly Brown Forman is going to ensure that a premium image is projected in everything about Slane. It understands brands after all.

The Conyngham family actually originate from Scotland arriving at Slane some 300 years ago via Donegal. One of the family's claims to fame was that Elizabeth, the first Marchioness Conyngham, was a mistress to King George IV who visited the castle in 1821. They were also heavily involved in another pastime for which Ireland is famous - horse racing. From the mid-19th century, the Conynghams became leading owners of top quality Irish thoroughbreds. The 2nd Marquess was actively involved in the Turf Club and sponsored the Conyngham Cup and the Slane Cup at Punchestown. Over the years they have produced many famous race winners including that of the 1860 Grand National.

Indeed any tour of Ireland has to mention the population's love of horses. In researching this book, I was accompanied for a while by a racing journalist friend who organised for us to take in the Punchestown Festival amidst our golf and whiskey visits. It's a marvellous event with a terrific atmosphere attended by passionate and knowledgeable people. But what I noticed more was the level of interest across the country. During the week of the festival we travelled onto the west coast and everywhere we met people and told them that we had been at Punchestown they expressed genuine interest and excitement and often strong opinions on what had happened or what they thought would happen the following day. When big race meetings are on in Ireland, they are national events, very much part of the national psyche. Golf and whiskey are both becoming increasingly popular in Ireland but I sense that neither have the same breadth and depth of following as horse racing.

Distilling began in 2018 so whiskey produced from the new distillery will not be available until 2021. Until then Slane Whiskey will be outsourced and is a blend made from malted and unmalted Irish barley. Its unique selling point is that it is not only triple distilled but 'triple casked' as it is a blend of spirit matured in virgin oak casks, bourbon barrels from Brown Forman and oloroso sherry casks. It's a pleasant mainstream dram which will fit well into Brown Forman's international portfolio and is likely to position itself as a competitor to Jameson. In addition to this blend there are plans for both a single malt and a single pot still whiskey.

Pennard Golf Club - 'The Links in the Sky'

There are magnificent views of the Gower Peninsula all around Pennard and this one from 6th green across Three Cliffs Bay is one of the best.

The Slane Distillery

The old Georgian stable buildings have been
lavishly and lovingly restored.

CHAPTER SEVEN

Ulster

'The chief object of every architect or greenkeeper worth his salt is to imitate the beauties of nature so closely as to make his work indistinguishable from Nature herself'

Alister MacKenzie (1870-1934)
The Spirit of St Andrews
Golf architect; designer of Augusta National,
Cyprus Point and many other great golf courses

ULSTER CAN BOAST one of Ireland's most famous whiskey brands and two of its greatest golf courses: Bushmills Whiskey and Royal County Down and Royal Portrush, both of which are generally ranked in the top 10 of UK and Ireland courses. While there are a number of new start-up distilleries emerging in Derry, Enniskillen and Newry, as well as Echlinville and Rademon in County Down which have been established for a few years, the choice of Bushmills was not difficult given its central role in the history of the Irish whiskey industry. Royal County Down and Royal Portrush are two of my favourite golf courses and the latter will become world famous after 2019 when it will host The Open after a gap of over 60 years, but both are too 'big' (and expensive) to meet my criteria. Instead I have chosen the less well known Castlerock, about half an hour along the coast from Bushmills.

It is worth starting by mentioning that coastline, as it is one of the most beautiful in the country and were it not for the political troubles, it would probably have become an even more popular tourist destination. Tourism, however, has increased significantly in recent years as there are many *Game of Thrones* film locations in the area. The most famous landmark is the dramatic Giant's Causeway with its unmistakeable basalt columns but there is much more besides from the Carrick-a-Rede rope bridge near Ballintoy, Rathlin Island, Dunluce Castle at Portrush, and the delightful Bann estuary.

Castlerock is situated on the western side of the Bann estuary and has two courses, the main 18-hole Mussenden Links and a second 9-hole layout, the Bann Course. The club opened as a 9-hole course in 1901 and was extended to 18 in 1906 when further land was leased. This design is credited to Ben Sayers, the Club Professional at North Berwick, a well-regarded golfer in his time who played regularly against many of the famous golfers of his day but whose best competition result was a tied second in The Open of 1888. He was perhaps not helped by his small stature as he stood just 5ft 3 inches tall. He was better known as an instructor, teaching not only fellow professionals such as Arnaud Massey, the first Frenchman to win The Open, but also the Prince of Wales, later George V, and also as a maker of golf balls and golf equipment. Ben Sayers went on to become a well-regarded brand of clubs made in a factory in North Berwick for many years until production moved to China in the 1980s.

Further modifications to the course are believed to have been undertaken by Harry Colt while he was working on nearby Portrush in the late 1920s while recently the club has commissioned Hawtree and Associates to do significant upgrades to six holes. This work was completed in 2018 shortly before my last visit. The good news is that these changes are subtle, mainly associated with the contours of the green, the positioning of bunkers and the design of links-style run off areas. I am confident that Alister MacKenzie would approve as the new changes are generally not visible and have been undertaken sympathetically, fitting in with the natural environment. Only the second hole has changed substantially as the green has been brought forward. When I visited, this green was still bedding in but the hole design, as a short uphill dog-leg Par 4, is inviting. This is a traditional links course and if anything the changes have been designed to accentuate its 'linksy' characteristics. For example, on 11 and 13, where the greens are close to the burn which runs across the course, they have addressed some drainage problems associated with clay soil in this area of the course.

The course is a Par 73, with five Par 5s, though the longest of these is just 510 yards so the overall course length is under 6,500 yards off the white tees. There are 6 par 4s of less than 400 yards but that does not make them easy; if they are into the wind they are long enough, while downwind shots, however short, are never easy on a links course. What I like about Castlerock is that there are so many interesting holes and that there is nothing predictable about it. Hole 6 is just 336 yards but, with a gentle dog-leg, the drive needs to be accurate and the second has to carry the burn which runs across short of the green. Maybe it was the Ben Sayers' influence but it reminded me of North Berwick with its infamous Eel Burn. 7

and 8, by contrast, are two longer Par 4s, generally into the prevailing wind, which require two accurate shots to get home. I must relay an incident on the 8th hole when I last played at Castlerock. I had been very pleased with myself having parred the stroke index 1 7th hole only to slice my drive into a bank on the 8th from where I somehow managed to hack it out of long grass back onto the fairway. I still had a long way to go for my third shot, blind, uphill into the wind. I topped it badly and it scuttled its way out of sight, though generally in the right direction. Meanwhile one of my playing partners hit his second from the middle of the fairway confidently in the air directly towards the green. As we walked up over the brow of the hill and looked towards the green, his ball could be seen some 12 feet left of the flag while my ball had done rather better than I had expected and was on the fairway about 15 yards short of the green. 'Could have been a lot worse', I thought to myself as I approached it, wondering whether to putt or chip as I needed to get down in two to prevent an ugly double bogey. I then noticed that this was in fact my partner's ball. Yes, my ball was the one 12 feet from the hole! His well struck shot had come up short, probably hit by the wind as it went up in the air, whereas my horrible mishit had been unencumbered by the elements and somehow scampered its way onto the green. Yes, obviously, I holed the putt for a par. It just says 4 on the scorecard. I walked off the green grinning. I could hear my playing partner chuntering.

When you next get an unlucky bounce or when a good shot is not rewarded, just remember that you will on occasion get a break of outrageous fortune. It may come in the same round; it may not. Some days you may get a few good breaks; others a few bad breaks. Accept it. It's golf. It's life.

That incident is a good reminder of why it really makes sense to make a very distinctive mark on your ball. It would have been easy to play my partner's ball as I was convinced that it was mine. Quite recently in a competition I drove the ball into the rough, walked into where I thought it had gone, found a ball with the same brand and number, played out the hole only to find on the next tee that my 'black dot' was missing. It was not my ball – the same brand and number but not mine. This was an unlucky coincidence but I hadn't checked properly. Perhaps if my ball had been more ostentatiously marked I would have noticed.

You can learn a lot about people in so many ways from playing golf with them. It is often said that it makes a very good job interview. There are so many clues to character and these are not just good and bad traits but clues as to the type of person. How someone marks their ball: some people scribble over it messily; others mark careful lines and dots. I know a very neat and tidy person who scribbles messily on her ball. How people dress: some are meticulously turned out in 'golf clothes'; others just wear clothes. Golf clothes, in particular trousers, have come in for a lot of comment over the years, particularly from non-golfers, with some justification. I am in the conservative camp – I don't have the self-confidence to do loud but admire those who do. I never forget playing at Machrihanish with my regular group and meeting an American dressed in the full Payne Stewart plus fours. It was not this so much, as the fact that the jersey and long socks were a matching, very bright, canary yellow 'tartan'.

Then there is the way that people react to fortune and

misfortune; some do so with equanimity while others will be more vocal. Like all good sports, golf is as much a mental test as a physical one. Clear thinking can make a huge difference. Over-thinking usually has a negative impact. Practice routines before hitting a shot can also give clues. There is no doubt that having some form of routine can help and all the professionals have this. I do think, however, that some amateurs can overdo it and this can also lead to slow play. There are others who prefer just to go up and hit the ball. I tend towards this camp. I think that can reflect these people's attitude to life and decision making. I haven't thought about whether the way someone decides on which whisky to have and how they drink it can also offer clues to character but perhaps I will watch for this.

The 9th hole is a long Par 3 aptly called 'Quarry' as the green nestles in a large hollow surrounded by dunes. You climb up to the 10th tee which is situated in the middle of the course and affords fine views in all directions. There is also a smart halfway hut which serves all types of refreshments.

Halfway huts are controversial and I am in two minds about them. I have enjoyed many of them over the years, the most notable being those at Swinley Forest, the New Zealand Club and Sunningdale where the sausage sandwiches used to be legendary. I can think of more modest ones at Royal Dornoch and Moor Park. Perhaps my favourite is at West Surrey, a slightly less well known but delightful Herbert Fowler designed course near Godalming. The hut neighbours the 8th green and there is a clear protocol that you order before you putt. This saves time and addresses the main objection to halfway huts, namely that they slow down a round. As a Scot, I was delighted to find at West Surrey that not only were the normal fillings of bacon, egg, sausage and mushrooms available in a breakfast bap, but also black pudding and haggis - or all of them together, if it were a particularly cold morning.

They clearly add time to a round so need to be managed well and, like at West Surrey, an agreed protocol understood by all. My view is that the issue of slow rounds is a separate one and it would be easy to save the five to ten minutes it takes at a halfway hut by playing at a sensible speed during the rest of the round. Halfway huts can add character to a course and can contribute to the overall golfing experience.

I will mention three holes on the back 9. The 10th is a relatively short dog-leg Par 4 where an extremely accurate drive is essential while the downhill second shot, usually with the wind behind, requires considerable thought and skill. The 17th is also downhill and a Par 5 with careful placement of both drive and second shot essential to enable a straightforward third into the green. The 18th is named 'Mussenden' and you can see the beautifully distinctive temple, which the course is named after and from which the club logo is derived, on the hillside beyond. The drive has a reasonably generous landing area though it helps to be in the right place for the second shot uphill to the green in front of the clubhouse. Here Hawtree has redesigned what was a simple two tier green into a fairer and more subtle sloping one. It's a strong finishing hole requiring an accurate second shot and careful putting on a tricky green.

The clubhouse sits up overlooking the course and has an excellent view of the course. Indeed the views on the course, particularly those at the end of the course overlooking the Bann estuary are exceptionally beautiful. You can see Portstewart, another fine course which has held The Irish Open, in the distance. The 9-hole Bann course is also worth playing. It is just 2,500 yards, comprising mainly relatively short par 4s, three Par 3s and one Par 5, but is a proper test of links golf.

Castlerock is to Portrush what Brora is to Dornoch, what Moray is to Nairn and what Panmure is to Carnoustie. They are all much easier and cheaper to play on and will probably, for the mid-handicapper, deliver a better overall experience. I hope that Castlerock will benefit from the likely increased interest there will be in Portrush and the recent upgrades to the course are timely in this respect. The club has a very engaging and active General Manager and we were treated delightfully as visitors. I will definitely go back to Castlerock.

Another place worth going back to is Bushmills Distillery. Situated in the attractive small village of Bushmills, just a few miles inland from the Giants' Causeway, it is ideally situated to benefit from any tourist boom. The brand markets itself with a confident statement that it is 'the world's oldest whiskey distillery'. Perhaps the 'e' is whiskey is important as that restricts 'the world' to largely Ireland and the US. Even within Ireland, Kilbeggan could perhaps lay claim to this distinction but I am not sure the debate is that fruitful. Indeed, when and where whisky, or whiskey, was invented rather depends on what you define as whisky. The product we know today - distilled spirit matured in wood for a number of years - is very different from the *uisce beatha* or *water of life* which whisky began as. Distilling of unmatured spirit can be traced back to Persian scholars, usually for medical purposes, while the Moors also distilled alcohol in Andalucia in the 10th century. Within Ireland, The Red Book of Ossery, written by a Franciscan monk at Kilkenny Cathedral in the 14th century contains early evidence of distillate recipes. It is likely that travelling monks contributed to distillation knowledge developing across Europe. The debate about whether Scotland or Ireland 'invented' whisky is further complicated by the fact that if you go back to the 5th Century AD some areas of each were part of the same kingdom. The kingdom of Old Dalriade existed before 'Scotland' and encompassed parts of modern Argyll, the southern Hebrides, including Islay, as well as parts of today's Antrim and Donegal and lasted some 400 years. I strongly recommend Fionnan O'Connor's scholarly book, *A Glass Apart*, which covers the origins of the Irish industry in some detail. There are many myths about Irish whiskey and what is different about it; some will say it is unpeated, some will point to triple distillation and some to the use of unmalted barley in the mash. All these are true only to some extent. While today, Irish blends are less peaty that is not a traditional characteristic of Irish whiskey as historically peat was used in both Scotland and Ireland. The use of peat or coal for malting was generally driven by local availability of fuel while the use of unmalted grains was again cost and availability driven. Triple distilling has been prevalent in the industry but was never universal. As we will see, what Irish whiskey is has changed as the industry has evolved and undergone periods of significant change.

Bushmills' claim is based on King James 1st granting a license to distil to Sir Thomas Philips, the local landowner and Governor of Antrim in 1608 though it is not until 1784 that the brand was registered. Bushmills benefited from the 19th century boom and the Victorian buildings of today's distillery date from the 1880s after a fire had destroyed the old distillery in 1885. To some extent Northern Ireland distillers at this time were more associated with Scotland than Ireland and there are shades of the political and religious divides. Ironically the success of the Scottish industry can be traced back to the invention by an Irish tax official, Aeneas Coffey, of the column or patent still (often known as a 'Coffey still') which was a much lower cost alternative to copper pot stills. This development of a continuous process for distillation was to revolutionise the industry. This indeed is the distillation process which most of the world's large Scotch blends use today as well as the major brands of bourbon, gin and vodka. While some semi-continuous distilling had been operating in the French brandy industry and the Scottish Stein business had also started using column stills in the 1820s, these early experiments struggled to produce a product of an acceptable quality. Learning from these, Coffey managed to perfect a process with two copper plated column stills to produce high quality clean spirit. In Ireland, Coffey's invention was widely regarded as a threat to traditional pot still produced whiskey while in Scotland and amongst the English gin distillers the new technology was quickly adopted. This enabled the Scottish industry and some of the Northern Irish players to develop two markets: the big re-distilling grain whisky market in England which was largely cost-driven, and blended Scotch, combining cheaply produced grain whisky with traditional malt to produce a lighter, more mainstream product which was to become the mainstay of the 20th century industry. By contrast, the Irish industry was slow to utilise this process believing that it did not produce the best flavour. Effectively the Irish did not follow this route until after the Second World War.

Bushmills has had a complicated ownership history.

Bushmills Distillery

Following the rebuilding in the late 1880s, Bushmills followed the success of its Scottish near neighbours and began to blend, becoming a popular export product winning international acclaim and a gold medal at the Paris Expo in 1889. The brand became well known (it is mentioned in Joyce's *Ulysses*) and was particularly popular in America. Once Prohibition ended it resumed exports there though the distillery was closed during the Second World War as the site was used for billeting troops. At that time Bushmills combined with the Coleraine Distillery which was subsequently closed. The brand was sold to the British drinks group Bass Charrington in the early 1970s but then was almost immediately acquired by Seagrams, a Canadian multinational business which was then one of the largest drinks companies in the world. Shortly afterwards,

Seagrams sold it to Irish Distillers in return for a 15 per cent stake in the whole company. This was the period when all the remaining Irish distilleries were in the same ownership. When Pernod Ricard acquired Irish Distillers over a decade later, they decided to focus on the Jameson brand and Bushmills was sold to Diageo. Diageo invested heavily and it was then a surprise to many industry commentators when Diageo in 2015 sold Bushmills to Casa Cuervo, a Mexican international drinks business. Effectively the businesses swapped brands; Diageo acquiring Casa Cuervo's premium tequila brand, Don Julio, in exchange for Bushmills.

Tequila is in fact quite an interesting and complex spirit not unlike malt whisky. It is derived from the blue agave plant and there are many different styles and brands. Quality can be dictated by where the agave is grown and whether 100 per cent agave is used and then different levels of maturation as with whisky.

Today the Irish whiskey industry has come full circle. It originated, as did Scotch, as a pot still product though with a tradition of using a combination of malted and unmalted barley and triple distilling. It is often said that the use of unmalted barley was due to tax avoidance as unmalted barley was untaxed. However, there is evidence that unmalted grains had been used for many years. Indeed wheat, oats and even potatoes would sometimes be included in recipes for early whiskies. The choice of grain was dictated by what excess grains were readily available in a particular year. However, the use of unmalted barley did evolve as an Irish tradition and is important in creating a distinctiveness in Irish Pot Still whiskey. Today's definition of 'Irish Pot Still whiskey' as opposed to 'single malt whiskey' is the requirement to use unmalted and malted barley - the triple distilling, on the other hand, is an Irish tradition but not a legal requirement. The invention by Aeneas Coffey of his patent still dramatically changed the whisky market enabling Scottish distilleries to prosper through developing blending and enabling them to survive the challenges of the early 20th century more successfully than their Irish counterparts. When Ireland finally embraced blending after the Second World War, the Jameson and Bushmills brands began to prosper both locally and internationally and today are best known for their mainstream blended offerings. The success of the Irish blends has provided the foundations for the recent industry revival and as the market develops and new enterprises are starting up, it is a renewed interest in Irish Single Malts and traditional Irish Pot Still whiskey that is now driving the growth. As Midleton (Jameson) re-introduced its Redbreast, Yellow Spot and Green Spot brands all focusing on Irish Pot still styles, so too Bushmills: as well as selling their standard Black Bush and new Red Bush blends, it is also experimenting with an increasing range of traditional single malts.

Significant investment has also gone into the visitor centre at Bushmills which has regular well populated tours, a large shop, tasting bar and restaurant. The old Victorian buildings have been expensively renovated. Inside the old wooden mash tun is used for demonstration purposes only with the new equipment being stainless steel. Bushmills has always had quite an innovative approach to distilling and there are seven stills and the distilling process at Bushmills seems quite complex. It continues a theme that I have learned during the writing of this book; there are many ways to distil a whisky and they will all deliver a slightly different result. No one way is right and no one way is wrong. There is no definitive 'best way'. It depends on what is wanted and the result is what any particular distillery produces. And distilling is just one of many other factors which combine to produce this most complex of products.

It says much about the history of the industry that the grain whiskey for the Bushmill blends comes from Midleton in Cork so the Bushmills brand is providing the malt whisky and the blending. Of course blended whisky can take many forms; the maturation of the grain whisky before blending can be relevant just as the maturation of the malt whisky with which it is blended. Then there are the relative quantities of each and what maturation is then undertaken. There are endless possibilities. Bushmills premium blend, Black Bush, for example, contains a high proportion of malt whisky which has been matured for some 11 years in sherry casks before it is blended with grain whiskey. It is likely that the market for 'premium blends' will also increase at prices between mainstream blends and mainstream single and Irish pot still malts.

Bushmills is the great survivor of the Irish industry and this is partly due to its geographic and cultural proximity to Scotland which meant that it more closely followed the Scottish industry path than that of its native Ireland. The difference with Bushmills is that the one brand stretches across mainstream blends and, increasingly, quality single malts, something which does not generally happen in Scotland.

CHAPTER EIGHT

Donegal

'Many interesting and curious facts might be related of the extraordinary contrivances of the people to evade the law and prevent detection, such as the artful construction of distilleries on the boundaries of townlands, in the caverns of mountains, on islands in lakes, on boats in rivers; of carrying away and secreting revenue officers for weeks together to prevent their giving testimony, the romantic manner of their treatment while in confinement, and the various other schemes and devices to defeat the intentions of the Government'

Alfred Barnard (1837-1918)
The Whisky Distilleries of the United Kingdom

I WENT ON holiday to Donegal as a child in the late 1960s. This was before what became known as 'the troubles'. We lived in the Scottish Borders and would load my father's car (a Humber Super Snipe) with suitcases on a roof rack and set off to take the ferry from Stranraer to Larne from where we would drive across to Donegal. There were only two place names which I remembered from those days; Kilybegs, which I somehow associated with kippers, and Rathmullen which I associated with a large hotel by a beach. Returning to Donegal was therefore something I wanted to do.

I knew that there were golf courses aplenty. From Murvagh at Donegal Town itself in the west to Ballyliffen on the Inishowen Peninsula in the north east, plus many in between, there is no shortage of options. Whiskey though was more difficult and left me with a dilemma; at the time of my research no whiskey was being distilled in Donegal. However, there were plans for a whiskey distillery in the small town of Carrick in western Donegal where they were already producing a very successful gin. It had to be investigated.

Donegal is beautiful. It is not the same beauty as the south and west of Ireland nor is it similar to Antrim. If Donegal reminds me of anywhere it is Scotland and maybe that is why it appeals so much. There is not the drama of Kerry and the Macgillycuddy's Reeks or the rugged Galway coastline, nor the empty plains of the centre of Ireland where the landscape can, to be blunt, look very uninviting. There is, however, moorland with heather and peat bogs, rolling hills with glens and valleys with loughs, while the coastline is endlessly varied.

There are many contradictions to Donegal; while it is part of the Irish Republic, geographically it is north of most of Northern Ireland with Malin Head on the remote Inishowen peninsula the most northerly point on the Emerald Isle. It is the fourth largest Irish county by area but has a population of just 160,000. It is also one of the strongest areas for the Irish Gaelic language. The largest town is Letterkenny with just under 20,000 inhabitants; Donegal Town itself is not much more than a large village with a population of less than 3,000 while the County town, Lifford, is even smaller. So there are no motorways and no major industry though Donegal has a history of producing high quality textiles. Again, maybe here I can sense an affinity; my father ran a woollen mill in the Scottish Borders, an area with a proud history of textile making.

It is not very accessible and that is probably why it is different. Donegal airport is in the middle of Donegal but isn't near anywhere. You can fly there only from Glasgow or Dublin. But if you get the chance, do so. You won't be disappointed.

Donegal has a long, some may say proud, history of illegal distilling with its remoteness, rather like the Scottish Highlands, providing some protection from the excisemen. Barnard's description at the beginning of this chapter was referring to activities across many areas of both Scotland and Ireland but it was in remote areas like Donegal where it was most prevalent. The last known legal distilling was in 1841 when a legal distillery near Letterkenny closed. Donegal did not participate in the late 19th century boom for Irish whiskey and, as we know, the 20th century proved challenging for the whole industry. So why choose Donegal for a new venture? My answer would be 'Why not?' and the landscape and climate certainly lend itself to the process. Choosing a distillery which has not yet been built may seem strange but it is such an interesting and heart-warming story that it merits telling. Start-ups are never easy and the story of the challenges which this distillery has faced makes a fascinating case history.

The vision is that of James and Moira Doherty. James, who has strong family routes in Donegal, and his wife Moira, Zimbabwean by birth, uprooted their family from Hong Kong in late 2014 where James had worked for the international drinks business SAB Miller, to move to Donegal with a plan to build a distillery. As well as his SAB Miller experience, James had worked for William Grant so knew his whisky. They moved to Carrick where his family had lived. It is worth pointing out that within remote Donegal, Carrick is one of the more remote villages, just a few miles from the most westerly point of the county. This is real, deep Donegal and they decided to call their distillery after Sliabh Liag (pronounced *slieve league*), a coastal mountain a few miles away which creates, at over 600 metres, some of the highest and most spectacular cliffs in Europe. If they were not as remote, these would be a huge visitor attraction, like the more famous Cliffs of Moher further south in County Clare. It took just over a year for a site to be identified on the outskirts of the village, for plans drawn up and planning permission to be sought. Meanwhile, to help cash flow, they launched an outsourced blended whiskey called The Silkie and rented a site on the southern outskirts of the village where in 2017 they installed a small gin still to produce a very high quality gin called An Dulaman. This also allowed them not only to generate cash by selling the gin but also to host tours to take visitors through the gin making process and talk about the plans for the distillery. It is all very personal, very informal. An Dulaman is described as an 'Irish Maritime Gin' made with eleven botanicals including five locally harvested varieties of seaweed. Their process is unashamedly artisan producing a proper 'London Dry' gin, distilling in a narrow temperature band and taking a very narrow cut from each distillation. They position it as a 'super premium' gin with each bottle wax sealed with a batch number linked to the lunar phases.

The project also had the backing of Oliver Hughes, a well-known figure in the Irish whiskey industry who was also involved in our next distillery visit at Dingle. Hughes was a lawyer by training and became a drinks entrepreneur spotting initially the craft beer movement and then setting up a chain of good value pubs with branches not just in Ireland but also London and New York. He was early to spot the opportunity for premium artisan spirits and in 2012 founded the Dingle Distillery where we are headed next. Sadly for the Irish whiskey industry, Hughes died of a heart attack in 2016 at the age of only 57. This must have been a big blow to the Dohertys as Hughes had been an enthusiastic supporter of this ambitious entrepreneurial enterprise.

Mussenden Temple

The Dohertys learnt of Oliver's untimely death just as they had received planning permission for their new distillery. So why, when I visited in 2018, was there no sign of a new distillery? Despite receiving the planning permission there was a local dispute as to the ownership of the land. It seems that a small group within the community were not supportive of the project and managed to delay and frustrate the plans. Eventually the Dohertys could wait no longer and approached the council in Ardara, 15 miles to the north, agreed a site and made the very difficult decision to relocate the project. This has been a serious shock to most of the community of Carrick who had been supportive and were looking forward to the estimated 40 jobs which would have been created.

I find it difficult to fathom why anyone would oppose the setting up of a quality artisan business in a remote community. And it only goes to prove that entrepreneurs need to have patience and resilience. Planning issues can always frustrate start-ups - there were similar issues at The Lakes Distillery, The English Whisky Company in Norfolk and Dartmoor Whisky in Bovey Tracey. They knew that planning permission would be a challenge and so ensured that they had a high quality design which the local community could accept. But, as ever in life, it is the unexpected which occurs.

I'm sure that the move to Ardara is something of a disappointment as it takes them away from his ancestral village and geographically a little further away from Sliabh Liag. However, there are probably some upsides. Ardara is a small but incredibly bustling town with hotels, bars and restaurants. It is only half an hour away but will be more accessible to Donegal visitors. It does, incidentally, take the distillery much closer to my chosen golf course. While I have not seen the new site in Ardara, I do not think the new location will in any way compromise the potential for the business. It is unlikely to be in quite as pretty a setting though the drive between Carrick and Ardara is an incredibly scenic one as you climb and get a view back over what looks like the whole of Donegal. What is most sad is the loss to the community at Carrick. They are the losers I'm afraid though it would be good if the distillery can maintain some sort of presence in the town.

The Silkie Whiskey is a pleasant blend and readily available in local bars in Donegal as is the gin. I am not a gin expert but this one did taste very distinctive - they have certainly gone for quality both in their choice of botanicals and in their process. The plan will be to move the gin still alongside the new whiskey distilling in due course. When they start producing whiskey the flagship product will be a single malt but there will also be an Irish Pot Still whiskey (both under the Sliabh Liag brand). They plan for these to be modelled on traditional Donegal whiskies though quite how they know what these really tasted like, I am not sure. They are looking for 'a rich, dry, smoky' flavour which suggests a traditional 'Scottish' style malt. Maturation will use a 'solera' system which again reflects the Irish heritage of using sherry barrels. They will bring to the market limited releases at different ages, as all start-ups are doing, but unlike some they plan to create a 'signature' 10-year-old single malt. They will also release a 'Donegal straight Poitin' under the brand An Béal Bocht, which means 'the poor mouth', in deference to Donegal's illustrious reputation for illegal distilling. Other distilleries are also releasing 'poitin' which, as it doesn't have to conform to any particular regulatory conditions, can be rather a risk to the consumer. As historically poitin was made from whatever excess grains and cereals were available this can be said to reflect the product's traditions. Some are distilled from a mixture of not just barley but anything from potatoes to sugar beet while others are simply cask strength 'young' whiskies.

This product range - a blend, a single malt, an Irish Pot Still and a poitin - for an Irish start-up makes sense as it encompasses everything of Irish whiskey's complex history. The early industry up until the 1823 Excise Act was dominated by illegal 'poitin' distillers particularly in remote areas like Donegal. As the legal industry boomed in the late 19th century, Irish Whiskey developed a distinctive premium quality product, namely Irish Pot Still whiskey, using a mash of both unmalted and malted barley. Then after the almost terminal decline of the industry in the first half of the 20th century it was milder blends which led the revival. Meanwhile the Scottish industry has thrived internationally with the growth of premium single malt whiskies and Bushmills and the new Irish start-ups are also producing this style of product. It is interesting that the Sliabh Liag website suggests that the 10-year-old single malt will be the flagship line as opposed to the more distinctively Irish, Irish Pot Still whiskey.

The golf course which I have chosen is Narin and Portnoo just a short fifteen minute drive from Ardara. Before talking about it though I should mention the other magnificent courses in Donegal because any of them would merit a feature and all would qualify in terms of my criteria. Starting in the west, there is Donegal Golf Club at Murvagh. The club moved to this beautifully peaceful location in a Special Conservation Area south of the town in 1973 with the course designed by Eddie Hackett with subsequent modifications by Pat Ruddy. The views are delightful in every direction. It is designed in the 'Muirfield format' of two concentric loops, one clockwise and the other anti-clockwise. It is also a long course being nearly 7,500 yards off the back tees. The modern clubhouse is welcoming.

Rosapenna, situated on the north coast on Sheephaven Bay, has two fantastic courses. The original one was designed by no less than Old Tom Morris who travelled there in 1891. His course consisted of two nines, one being a traditional links and the other being less so as it occupied higher ground the other side of the road. This 9 has now been replaced by a more links-like second 9, designed again by Pat Ruddy, next to the original. The main course today however is a new links, Rosapenna Sandy Hills, built in some magnificent dune land alongside. Designed also by Eddie Hackett, it is a great example of a modern links and the views are spectacular in every direction. Further east is Portsalon which has to be regarded as a real hidden gem. It is less well known and I had modest expectations. How wrong I was. It is a magnificent course and a real test of golf. Although some recent modifications have been made under the guidance of former Ryder Cup captain, Paul McGinley, the main upgrade to the course opened in 2002 and was the work of Pat Ruddy. There are numerous strong holes, perhaps most noteworthy being the 2nd which has a Machrihanish 1st, risk and reward type drive but, if anything, is more fearsome, being elevated. The second shot also has a burn in front of the green. I was delighted to mark a five on my card – a slightly conservative drive followed by my favourite club selection of 'two 9 irons'. I didn't fancy the 200 yard second over the burn. Again it is beautiful, laid out alongside a wonderful beach.

Finally there is Ballyliffen where, like at Rosapenna, an old links has been revived and joined by a brand new design next door. Again we encounter both Hackett, who was involved in reviving the Old Course, and Ruddy who largely designed the new Glashedy which held the Irish Open in 2018. The wonderful weather for the first three days must have been a godsend for the Irish Tourist Board. If I'm sounding boring again talking about the views I don't apologise. Just go and see them.

I haven't mentioned, and haven't played, a 9-hole course called Cruet Island which looks a worthy companion to this illustrious list. Donegal really can compete with some of the other clusters of golfing excellence around the UK coastline; Fife, East Lothian, Lancashire, South Wales and Kent.

So to Narin and Portnoo; these are two neighbouring villages in a magnificent setting overlooking the beaches of the wide Gweebarra Bay. There is evidence of golf being played in the area on a number of 9-hole layouts from the late 19th century but none seemed to survive the Great War and the current club was not formed until 1930 so it is not as ancient as many other links courses. Its history has at times also been difficult. There have been two significant modifications to the layout, first in 1965 when it first became 18 holes and subsequently in 2004 which the current routing dates from. But this is not the end of the story. The club was faced with closure in late 2017 and was bought in early 2018 by two Irish American businessmen, one a Donegal native who had enjoyed childhood holidays in a caravan at Narin and Portnoo. They have commissioned the renowned American architect Gill Hanse to upgrade the course. They are adamant that the plan is not to make it into a high-end resort course but to make the most of the beautifully natural links terrain.

I am cautiously optimistic because Narin and Portnoo is

not perfect. It probably isn't the best course in Donegal though it has some of the best holes with the stretch from 5-11 often described as the best 'seven hole stretch in Ireland'. I would not disagree and there are some other good holes besides. The course starts modestly with a short par 4 where the main challenge is the second shot to a tricky green where you will want to leave yourself an uphill putt. 2, 3 and 4 are situated on flat land on the inland side of the dunes and are as a result unremarkable. 18 suffers from the same problem and lacks definition. I assume that Gil Hanse will focus on these holes because I would leave much of the rest well alone. The excitement starts with the second shot at the 5th where you hit uphill to a green on the edge of the dunes. The 6th is a dramatic dog-leg with a blind drive to a fairway riven with deep valleys and again the second shot plays uphill into the dunes. The 7th is a great Par 3 across a valley to a green which is more generous than it looks but which you don't want to miss in any direction. 8 then plays downhill and the second shot to the green perched above the beach is fearsomely tricky; running it in is awkward because of the terrain but holding the ball on the green can also be difficult, especially with the wind behind. There is little protection from the beach behind the green. 9 plays along the shoreline over a hill again to a beautifully situated green above another beach. The views on this stretch of the course are simply delightful, not only along the coast and out to sea but also inland where there are numerous inlets and small bays with yet more empty beaches. 10 is a Par 5 that starts off innocently but the green is separated from the fairway by nasty gully to the front and left. 11 is then a tough long Par 3 which is all carry. This is unquestionably a great series of holes. 12 takes you back towards the flatter ground and plays somewhat uninterestingly along the inside side of the dunes up to the green. There then follows three Par 5s, all of which are good links holes with narrowing fairways as you approach the greens. The last of them, the 15th, is also scenically beautiful as it plays along the top of the dunes with a vast expanse of beach to the side and ahead.

A word about the clubhouse; the old wooden construction was replaced in 1967 and the building reflected the rather disappointing architecture of that age. However, in 2008, a new front was added to it giving a generous bar and lounge with views over the 1st and 18th. I visited in the summer after the course had been taken over and the greeting and service were exceptional with young and enthusiastic bar staff. My homemade chowder with fresh bread was perfect. This makes a huge difference to visitors and if the new American owners have instilled some modern service culture then that is to be applauded. The whole experience was very positive. For a course which is not well known and does not have the famous history of others, they will need to rely on word of mouth so ensuring that every visitor is treated as special will be very important. I remember playing other courses where I have enjoyed the golf but felt that the club were simply taking my money and not that bothered about looking after me. Generally this is not the case in Ireland as the Irish are well known for their bonhomie and in my many visits I can remember much friendly banter. I have to relate one story from a visit to a course on the west coast. There were six of us playing in two threeballs and, as we did not know the course, we had decided to order a caddy for each group. The conversation went as follows:

'Could we please book two caddies for our round?'

'Yes, of course, would you like four caddies?'
'Er, no we would just like one for each group.'
'OK. Four caddies?'
No, we are playing in two threeballs so two will do'
'Yes, that's fine. Two four caddies'

It was only at this point that I realised that he was talking about 'fore' caddies which are caddies that simply carry your bag and tell you where to go as opposed to giving advice on shots. To this day I don't know whether it was his Irish sense of humour having fun at my expense or whether the misunderstanding was genuine.

I left Donegal with a determination to return soon. Within the one county there are at least half a dozen great golfing locations but it requires about five hours of driving to start at Ballyliffin in the north east and take in Portsalon, Rosapenna, Cruit Island, Narin and Portnoo and end up at Donegal golf club in the south west. My advice is to take your time and savour the beauty of the environment, the magnificence of the golf courses and soon you will be able to add to this by savouring the warm delights of a dram of Sliabh Liag whiskey at the end of each day.

Narin and Portnoo Golf Club

There are beach views in every direction from Narin and Portnoo. This one is from the 16th tee and is of the main beach of the two neighbouring villages, Narin and Portnoo. It is a delightful example of the beauty of the Donegal coastline.

Skellig Michael

The Skellig Islands became a UNESCO World heritage Site in 1996. There is an ancient monastery on the southern peak but today it is mainly inhabited by a remarkable number of seabirds and other fauna and flora; as well as grey seals and a colony of razorbills, there is said to be an eyrie of peregrine falcons, fulmars, Manx sheerwaters, storm petrels, gannets, guillemots and Atlantic puffins.

CHAPTER NINE

Kerry

*'The light music of whisky falling into glasses
made an agreeable interlude.'*

James Joyce (1882-1941)

The Dubliners.

FOR OUR FINAL destination, we head towards the south west of Ireland. From Donegal this invites a drive down the 'Wild Atlantic Way', a route now heavily marketed by the Irish Tourist Board, which takes in the entire west Ireland coastline which is certainly 'wild' in many places. The simple three 'w's logo now adorns road signs all the way down the west of Ireland. It may be only about 250 miles from Donegal town to Cork but a direct drive will take about five hours while if you followed the Wild Atlantic Way you would need at least a week.

Great golf courses are not in short supply along the way staring with the famous County Sligo at Rosses Point, the recently much improved Enniscrone, along to Carne on the far north western tip of the Galway peninsula, down to Lahinch then Doonbeg, Ballybunion and Tralee. These are all must play courses for any links golf enthusiast. Most are not only great (and I mean great) golf courses but again their settings are often spectacular - Rosses Point, Ballybunion, Doonbeg and

Tralee score highest on this count.

There are signs too of the whiskey revival along this route. The Connaught Whiskey Company in Ballina and the Nephin Whiskey Distillery situated under the majestic mountain of the same name in County Mayo, are already distilling while there are plans for distilleries at Lough Gill outside Sligo and further south in the Burren in County Clare. Heading though to the south west of Ireland, there is a case for making Cork the base and visiting Midleton, the heart of the Irish whiskey industry. Midleton has played the central role in the industry's history and today, as well as its internationally famous branded blends, it is also, with its Redbreast, Green Spot and Yellow Spot brands, playing an important leadership role in the current revival of Irish Pot Still whiskies. The new distillery has an impressive visitor centre and is definitely worth a visit. I have, however, gone elsewhere for two reasons. Cork is a pleasant city but hardly matches the delights of nearby County Kerry and I was keen to explore another new venture rather than an existing one.

The two best known golf courses in Kerry are Waterville and Tralee. Both have American influence. Golf started at Waterville towards the end of the 19th century as the area was famous for being the European end of the first transatlantic cable. The station can still be visited today. The 9 hole course was popular though the cable station closed after the Second World War as new technology took over and the course declined. In 1967, an Irish born American, John Mulcahy, bought the course and commissioned Eddie Hackett to extend it to 18 holes and, together with a new clubhouse, the new course was opened in 1973. In 1987 the club was again sold to a group of Americans who also bought a nearby hotel and fishery as well as commissioning Tom Fazio to upgrade the course. It is now a popular destination for American golfers. Tralee Golf Club dates from 1896 but the course was a 9-hole layout near the town. In 1984 the club moved several miles up the coast to Barrow where a new links was created, designed by Arnold Palmer. Today it is a thriving club and remains, in contrast to Waterville, an Irish club. Of the two courses, Waterville is usually the higher rated but I much prefer Tralee. It has two 9-hole loops, one to the south of the beautifully situated clubhouse and one to the north. The first 9 is pleasant with an interesting variety of holes. The second nine, and in particular 11-17, is quite simply awe-inspiring. Actually, I think holes 11-17 beat Narin and Portnoo for the best stretch of seven holes in Ireland. They really do take the breath away in their beauty, their ingenuity and as a serious test of golf. The 11th is a big Par 5 where you drive to the bottom of a steep slope from where you have to play your second uphill between two huge dunes. 12 is one of the most terrifying holes in golf. The drive is blind and downhill and needs to be accurate as the fairway narrows and runs off to the left. The second shot is to a green perched on the side of a massive dune with a dramatic cliff edge to the left. You simply can't miss left but if you bale out right you will find yourself in a difficult position with the danger of falling down the bank with your third. Trust your swing and aim for the right hand side of the green. In theory it's simple. 13 is a Par 3 to another green perched against a high dune. You have to hit the green – there is little else. The 14th tee has spectacular views and the drive is down to a split fairway; the higher, narrower section will give you an easier second, from where you need a controlled shot downhill to hit the green. 15 turns back along the coast and is a tricky short Par 4 requiring accuracy with both shots to hit a slightly hidden green nestling amongst the dunes overlooking the sea. 16 is a magnificent Par 3 playing down along the coastline to a green on a steep slope against the shoreline. 17 then plays back uphill with an accurate drive required between bunkers and then a steep uphill second to a mercifully fairly flat green. It is almost a relief that the 18th is a fairly straightforward Par 5 back to the clubhouse. And yes, the views across bays and beaches (Ryan's Daughter was filmed nearby) add hugely to the experience. Tralee could well be my favourite course in Ireland and I am surprised that so many courses are rated above it.

So 5-11 at Narin and Portnoo or 11-17 at Tralee; which is best seven hole stretch? Now that I have invented the concept of the 'best 7 hole stretch', I am thinking of others. I think they need to be distinctive in some ways and represent a stretch of holes which stand out within the overall context of that course. Perhaps 2-8 at Royal Aberdeen would qualify? 9-15 at Swinley Forest? They are possibly not distinctive enough within the overall quality of that course. Maybe 1-7 at North Berwick or indeed 11 to 17 at North Berwick would qualify. 1-7 at Portstewart certainly would. I am sure avid golfers will be able to think of their own.

Yet, I am not going to feature Tralee because there are other courses to visit. Dooks is situated near Glenbeigh at the southern corner of Dingle Bay overlooking the remarkable promontory of Inch Beach which sticks out into the bay from the northern side. The club has a history dating back to 1889 when 9 holes were laid out by the Royal Ordnance Corps. A further 9 holes were added ten years later but these were subsequently abandoned and it didn't return to 18 holes until the 1960s. Today's course, however, dates from a major overhaul by Martin Hawtree which opened in 2006. While 'Dooks' takes its name from the Irish word 'doaughs' meaning 'dunes', the dunes are of the subtle rather than dramatic variety. Indeed everything about this course is pleasantly understated. The setting is delightfully peaceful and it is one of few clubs which has a page on its website devoted to the environment, talking through the fauna and flora which you will find on the course. Appropriately the club's logo is a natterjack toad. I think all golf clubs should show this level of respect for their environment.

Dooks is therefore another 'must visit' on our way to our final destination, Dingle, where we can finish our tour with a visit to the UK and Ireland's most westerly distillery and most westerly golf course. Dingle often gets missed by tourists to County Kerry who stick to the scenic Ring of Kerry drive with its spectacular views over the wonderfully named Magillicuddy Reeks mountain range. The Dingle peninsula is about 30 miles long with Dingle town about four fifths of the way along but you will need to leave an hour from the main road to get there.

Dingle is a small fishing town but a bustling one. It has a pretty harbour front and there are plenty of bars and restaurants. There is a famous music festival and the annual Dingle Races, if not quite having the same prestige as Punchestown or the Curragh, is the biggest horse and pony racing event in the country. There are many small hotels and decent quality bed and breakfast options plus a good choice of seafood restaurants. It's a very pleasant place to stay.

It was here that in 2012 a new whiskey distillery was created in an old sawmill on the western edge of the town. I wanted to feature Dingle not because it is just another example of a start-up which has contributed to the revival of the Irish whiskey industry but because it was the first to do so. It was the pioneer and set the trend for what has followed both by other entrepreneurial start-ups but also the big players who have recognised the potential for Irish whiskey. By the time it had released its first batch in December 2015, the revival of the industry had begun and many new Irish whiskey brands had already been created but most were blends and of course they were all contract distilled, mainly from Cooleys. Hughes set the trend but with the lead time for building new distilleries and the subsequent three year wait for maturing, it will be into the 2020s before significant stocks of new brands appear.

It was the brainchild of Oliver Hughes together with his business partner from his Porterhouse Drinks Group, Liam Lahart, and Peter Mosley. The start-up was partly financed by a 'founding fathers' investment scheme, the names of whom are proudly displayed in a wooden wall in the distillery. The untimely death of Oliver Hughes only months after the first release of whiskey was a huge blow to the project yet it has established itself as the definitive artisan Irish whiskey brand. However, Hughes had hired plenty of whisky experience and his son Elliot is now involved. The plan remains to stay unashamedly artisan, limiting volume and releasing limited quantities which keeps the premium pricing– early releases sold for €350 a bottle. At times it was impossible to buy any product. At time of writing in 2018, Batch 3, a bourbon and port cask single malt, has been released with initial prices quoted of over €100 a bottle though it can be obtained on some websites at around €80 a bottle. This is still an impressive premium and clearly export, particularly America, will be an important market. This batch won 'Best new Irish whiskey' at the Irish Whiskey awards where they also won the award for best Irish gin. Later in 2018, they released a 2nd batch Single Pot Still whiskey matured in bourbon, sherry and port barrels. Again it is commanding a premium price.

The website clearly states their proposition – 'we are not in the business of creating megabrands….our scale is modest.' The distillery has three whiskey stills for triple distilling, a mash-tun and five washbacks. The three Forsyth's stills have a 'boil ball' design to encourage reflux and thereby produce a cleaner spirit. Again, we encounter in these new start-ups a passion for the art of distilling.

While there is no smart visitor centre, there are regular tours which seem to be well patronised – I visited in April and needed to book as the tour was full with a wide range of nationalities. The tour is very informal and they are not licensed to sell product from their small shop. The only tasting we got was of the gin which has been an unexpected success and is now an important part of the business plan. They have created a very distinctive bottle shape for the gin and vodka which features a reproduction of a painting by a local artist, Honora O'Neill, called 'the Spirit of Dingle'. It is of the delightful view from the distillery down the bay towards the town. The original hangs in the Fraunces Tavern in New York, a pub and museum which is part of the Porterhouse Brewing Company. Honora O'Neil has a small gallery in Dingle but lives on the very western edge of the Dingle peninsula from where she gets her inspiration to paint beautiful seascapes. They also sell a premium vodka.

I have to express some disappointment in my last two visits in that in neither did I get to taste any whiskey which hasn't given me the opportunity to sum up the differences between Scotch and Irish whiskey. The story, as you will have learned, is much more complicated than I had realised because those differences have changed over the years. I explained in *Of Peats and Putts* that there were five types of Scotch whisky - single and blended malts, single and blended grains and blended malt and grain, though both single and blended grain whiskies are rare. The biggest market by far is for blends of malt and grain and this is the same in Ireland. Irish blends are slightly milder, slightly sweeter than Scotch ones, perhaps more akin to American whiskies. Irish single malts are relatively new and simply add to the huge diversity which you get in Scotland. What Ireland has which is different is Irish Pot Still whiskey which uses unmalted as well as malted barley in the mash. This was the product which made the Irish industry famous in the late 19th century but which was also the product which was overtaken by the Scottish blends after the development of the patent still. The revival of the Irish industry did not begin with the re-emergence of this product but with Irish whiskey distillers producing their own blends which they marketed as milder and sweeter than Scotch. Instead of going back to their traditions they successfully jumped on the blended bandwagon. As the Jameson brand became successful internationally and led the revival of the Irish industry, the 'real' Irish Pot Still product almost disappeared. To its credit, it was also Midleton that instigated the revival of Irish Pot Still products with the re-introduction of lines under its Redbreast and Yellow Spot brands during the early 1990s thereby re-kindling interest in this real representative of Irish Whiskey.

So while I was unable to taste in either Dingle or Donegal, I did take the opportunity to try traditional Irish Pot Still products (mostly Midleton produced Redbreast and Yellow Spot) and they are definitely different. I stress that my palate remains quite uneducated but the more you try, the more you learn. The well-known Scottish whisky writer, Charles Maclean, explains that whisky is not only about the taste but a combination of smell, taste and texture. With Irish Pot Still whiskey it is perhaps the texture more than anything which you notice as the unmalted barley gives it a smooth, oily (in a pleasant way) mouthfeel. I don't believe that triple distilling in itself is a major differentiator. Some Scottish malts triple distil (e.g. Hazelburn and Auchentoshen) and triple distilling is just another way of distilling and as we have seen there are many innovations already happening in the distilling process. So if you want something distinctively Irish, look out for Irish Pot Still whiskey.

The Dingle Golf Club, properly known as Ceann Sibeal, is not in Dingle but further along the Dingle peninsula, about a 20 minute drive north west from the town. It is not only the most westerly golf course in the British Isles but the most westerly in Europe (not counting Iceland as part of Europe). It is certainly remote and when you get there it feels remote. The course is a very traditional links though it doesn't quite border the sea. It lies in a big bay area surrounded by hills which form a large semi-circular frame to the views to the south. To the west there are views out to sea with the distinctive shapes of the Skellig Islands clearly visible just off the coast and the Blasket Islands in the distance. Skellig Michael, as well as being a UNECSO world heritage site and a haven for a vast range of bird life and puffins in particular, is also famous for featuring in the most recent Star Wars films. The setting is restful and peaceful with a strong sense of remoteness. There is also a sense of scale; the day I visited in late April, the weather was changeable and one of the attractions was watching the weather change across the vast panorama of hills which frame the setting. There was a lot of weather about and you could watch it moving across the surrounding hills; showers here, bursts of sunshine there, sometimes reaching the course and sometimes just passing by in the distance. You felt as if you were on the 'Wild Atlantic' coast and on the most westerly tip of the British Isles.

Ceann Sibeal has a pleasant clubhouse which has good views over the links; indeed it is so well located that you can see every hole on the course. I can't think of many clubhouses that can claim this. It is situated on a large sloping tract of land and the holes for the most part make their way up and down. The terrain is rarely flat and bland but there are no dunes so it lacks a bit of drama. No earth has been moved here to create interest; the attractions are of the more subtle variety with swales and gentle undulations on what is a very natural landscape. There are probably few strongly memorable holes yet with a constant wind and a combination of hole directions and changes in elevation, there is plenty of thought required. There is also a stream which runs across the course, and is crossed on no less than 11 of the 18 holes, which again gives the terrain an authentic, traditional links feel.

Despite this, it is not in fact an old course. The club was founded in 1924 and was initially based at two sites near Dingle until it was moved to the current location in the early 1970s.

It started as a 9-hole course (both its previous layouts near Dingle had been just 9 holes) and was an early design of Eddie Hackett. About ten years later it was extended to 18 holes with Christy O'Connor Junior being involved in the final design.

The quirky Dingle logo

It is perhaps time to pay tribute to Hackett and the influence he had on Irish golf course design. Hackett came from a modest background in Dublin and after getting a job at Royal Dublin became club professional at Royal Waterloo where he worked with Henry Cotton and then at Portmarnock. He only took up golf course design in later life but went on to create what are now regarded as many of Ireland's masterpieces:

Ballyliffen, Rosapenna Sandy Hills, Donegal, Enniscrone, Carne and Waterville as well as many lesser known ones besides. These courses vary in style from the dunes of Rosapenna and Waterville to the more natural landscapes of Ballyliffen and Dingle. I think 'natural' is the key ingredient of Hackett designs; he worked in Ireland in the 1970s and 1980s and, as he once said, worked with budgets more akin to those of Old Tom Morris than the new breed of American designers who were popular at the time. Moving great amounts of earth was not really an option so Hackett worked with what was there. If there were dunes he used them to great effect; if not he used the natural lie of the land. At Donegal Golf Club at Murvagh, there is a great section of the course in the dunes but also plenty of character elsewhere. At Ballyliffen the new course is dominated by the huge Glashedy hill which the course tracks up and down. So here at Ceann Sibeal there is the slope, the stream (or is it a burn?) and the natural swales of the links.

So while it is difficult to identify any outstanding holes, equally there are few weak ones. Generally the challenge is with the shots to the green which are often awkward. The greens are set in natural positions, not artificially raised, but usually protected by some feature of the lie of the land. Bunkering is relatively light but there are plenty other hazards to test the mind and demand certainty of shot. There is nothing contrived and that is what I like about the design; it is a true test of 'links golf' or 'the running game'.

I stated in *Of Peats and Putts* that I didn't like contrived hazards. Watching golf on the television at many newly designed courses around the world, so many of them look the same. There seems always to be a final hole with water up the left, dog-legging round so that the second shot plays over the water which nestles up against the green. It is not very subtle. It was the great Peter Thomson, winner of five Open Championships between 1954 and 1965, who referred to the scourge of 'gratuitous water' in golf course design. A well designed course doesn't have to look spectacular –indeed many of the great ones don't; Muirfield, Carnoustie, Lytham come to mind. Looking out over Ceann Sibeal from the clubhouse there is no 'wow' factor. The course, however, fits naturally into its surroundings and the test of golf is a genuine one.

I suppose I feel slightly torn. Tralee is a course which sets the heart racing. That is not the case at Ceann Sibeal. Tralee also has a more spectacular look to the course; you can see the coastline and the dramatic dunes and the prospect of the course wending its way amidst them whets the appetite. Again there is none of this at Ceann Sibeal though the setting is equally lovely. But to miss out on the delights of this special place, which so many visiting golfers do, is a shame. So you should play Tralee (and indeed Dooks) but make sure also that you plan a visit to Ceann Sibeal.

The same is true with my choice of whiskey destination. To visit Midleton is to visit the crucible of the industry, the place without which the industry could easily have disappeared. A visit to Midleton will tell you all you need to know about the history of the Irish whiskey. Yet Dingle too is I think symbolic of the future; a story of how a combination of entrepreneurial flair and a passion for the product can lead a revival of an industry. Maybe Midleton and Tralee are internationally better known but to end the tour experiencing the simple pleasures of Dingle and Ceann Sibeal feels appropriate.

Afterword

I RECENTLY WATCHED a very good documentary on Winston Churchill's passion for painting. In his lifetime he produced a remarkable 500+ canvasses some of which have sold recently for very significant sums. I should disclose that the documentary was by Andrew Marr, a school contemporary of mine. He talked about how painting was for Churchill an important therapy which allowed him to forget the troubles of life and fight the depression he often suffered from. Turning to painting he could become both possessed and free from life's anxieties. Marr felt empathy with this as he had also turned to painting to overcome troubles in his life, in particular a serious stroke which he had suffered a few years earlier.

Few of us go through life without experiencing troubles, difficulties, stresses. Today we understand much more the importance of good mental health, both in its own right but also as a contributor to good physical health. Alister MacKenzie in his remarkable book, *The Spirit of St Andrews*, wrote about why he abandoned his career in medicine to become a golf architect stating his firm conviction that golf had 'an extraordinary influence on health and pleasurable excitement, especially when combined with fresh air and exercise'. At the beginning of this book, I proposed a round of golf as a metaphor for life. I believe that golf, properly experienced, can, for some, offer that same therapy which Marr refers to with painting. I wish

I could paint, just as I wish I could play the piano, as I can understand how these activities could provide mental relief. For me, I can find therapy in golf - I can experience that 'joy to be alive feeling' - but not just any game of golf as the environment has to be right. That environment will include the type of course, the weather, the surroundings and the company. Unlike painting and playing music, therapeutic golf is not solitary but best enjoyed when accompanied. And like painting and music playing, no game of golf is ever perfect but the search for that perfection and the experience of those occasional moments of perfection can bring genuine satisfaction.

I suppose I should be careful in applying the same to whisky. Whisky is alcohol and so is a drug. But I believe that it can be a hugely beneficial drug. The reason for this lies in its complexity. Whisky is the most complex of drinks. It is definitely more complex than beer and rum and gin and even more complex than wine. I have used the word 'context' a lot but again I come back to it. Whisky cannot provide therapy in itself. Everything else has to be right. Not just the right type of whisky but also the occasion, the environment and the company. I'm not advocating drinking more quantity of whisky but instead revelling in the variety on offer.

And learning more about what it is that is contributing to that perfect environment for creating 'joy to be alive' golf playing and whisky drinking is what excites me; understanding more about types of grasses and greenkeeping methods and course designs; more about whisky distilling methods and maturing influences. I have learned that good golf courses are not just 'links' courses but that they are courses which offer the strategic challenge of 'the running game' and that this is usually to do with the type of grasses and the consequent quality of the turf as well as a 'naturalist' approach to hole design. I wish to explore this further. While in whisky, I have become increasingly intrigued by the multifarious factors which lie behind what the end product tastes like. I left Scotland believing that it was almost all in the maturation but now believe that, the use or otherwise of peat apart, there are different distilling processes which will impact on the end product. And increasingly I am judging my whisky not just by its taste but by its smell and texture too – perhaps Irish Pot Still whiskey in particular has helped me do this. As I learn and understand more, I know that I will enjoy it more.

Golf and whisky have both travelled easily outside of Scotland and both have global appeal. This book has looked at how they have travelled to the neighbouring parts of the British Isles. The answers are different. Golf travelled quickly south of the border from the 1890s and England and Wales now boast many great golfing locations. It is perhaps still not as much a central part of local communities as it remains in many parts of Scotland and indeed the future of many clubs is uncertain. There was a market boom in courses in the second half of the 20th century but many of these new courses, often built on unsuitable land, are struggling. Some of golf's complexities are not suited to today's life perceptions while it has suffered from the paradox of technology making it easier to play yet it now takes longer to do so. The new rules from 2019, which are designed to simplify (and hopefully speed up) the game, are welcome but it is too early to judge what impact they may have. Golf faces major challenges and I can't help thinking that the answer lies in returning to many of its origins; more, faster, two ball golf, more matchplay, less obsession with longer courses, more natural course designs, more use of fine grasses, more 9-hole courses and competitions. In a word, more 'fun'.

Whisky, on the other hand, is on the brink of a golden age. Despite alcohol consumption showing signs of declining, malt whisky consumption will grow. There is a clear correlation between the growth of aspiring middle classes around the world and the growth in whisky consumption and this will benefit both traditional whisky countries like Scotland and new ones like England, Wales and many other places around the world. Scotland does, however, have a brand reputation for whisky and Scotch will always remain the benchmark. The Royal and Ancient Golf Club at St Andrews which still runs the amateur game needs to look to secure Scotland's central position as 'The Home of Golf' and promote the core values of the game.

Ireland is a different story as the histories of the development of both whiskey and golf have been inextricably tied up with the history of the island itself. The sad decline of the Irish whiskey industry in the 20th century very much reflected the tragic history of that country – the governing of Ireland by England from the Battle of the Boyne until independence is not a comfortable story and there remain legacies today. The history of the industry is fascinating and too complex for me to do it justice in this book. What is clear is that there have been and remain today many connections between the Scottish and Irish industries. Many of the great Dublin distilleries dating back to the 18th century were owned by Scottish businesses, such as the Haigs and the Steins. Even today one of Irish whiskey's most famous brands, Tullamore Dew, is owned by William Grant & Sons, owners of Glenfiddich, the world's biggest selling single malt. William Grant not only bought the Tullamore Dew brand but invested in a new distillery back in Tullamore – the original distillery had closed down in the 1950s and it had been contract produced elsewhere since then. It is perhaps also ironic that the patent still which was to revolutionise the Scottish industry and set the foundations for Scotch's worldwide reputation was invented by an Irishman and that the Scottish industry undoubtedly benefited from the decline of the Irish industry in the early 20th century.

But there are contradictions too. Scotch blends grew in the late 19th and early 20th century as they were milder and more appealing to a broader market than the stronger, harsher, Irish Pot Still whiskies. Today it has come full circle; Irish blends are smoother, milder versions of their Scottish counterparts. Scottish malts have found new markets; Irish malts and Irish Pot Still whiskies are now following that path.

Yet, the resurgence of the Irish whiskey industry in the 21st century also reflects the new confidence of Ireland, both north and south, since the Good Friday Agreement of 1997. Irish whiskey is the fastest growing sector of the world whiskey market. The same is true of golf; the boom in new golf courses and upgrading of old courses in Ireland has been happening for some thirty years. Courses like Narin and Portnoo and Portsalon which had been struggling are being upgraded and invested in. I think it is no coincidence that in the ten years from 2007, Ireland (north and south) boasted four major champions winning seven major titles; only the United States has a better record over this time period. Scotland, for example, has just two major winners in the past 40 years. Ireland has also provided three of the four European Ryder Cup Captains between 2014 and 2020.

What doesn't change, whether the whisky or the golf is in Scotland or England or Wales or Ireland is the endless fascination they both deliver, because they are always unpredictable and always enlightening. Every dram of whisky and every round of golf offers a different experience. I am reminded of a saying by the famous Spanish philosopher George Santayana: 'To be interested in the changing seasons is a happier state of mind than to be hopelessly in love with the spring'. This perfectly sums up my attitude to both golf and whisky. I don't want every dram of whisky to be the same. I don't want to drink the same one every time. I know that sometimes I will choose one and it will disappoint. Either it will not suit my taste or, for some reason, at that particular time, it will not quite satisfy. That might be my fault and not the whisky's. Equally though, at times a whisky will surprise. It will be magnificent. I will ask myself why I don't drink this one all the time. Then the next time it will be good but not quite as good. If every whisky were perfect every time you drank it, the whole drinking of whiskey would be a much less rewarding experience just as if every day brought perfect sunny weather you would soon lose the appreciation of that sunny weather.

So too with golf. The highs we all experience would not be so rewarding if they were commonplace. If every wedge shot from 100 yards landed near the pin the game would soon lose its appeal. I also don't want to play golf every day in perfect weather. It is good to play in different conditions. It is good that changes in the wind can radically alter the challenge. It is good that you sometimes get lucky bounces and sometimes unlucky ones. If every bounce were perfectly reliable it would be boring. This is why 'running game' courses are the most enjoyable.

These are universal truths about life and it is because both whisky and golf reflect these universal truths that they both have global appeal. I have learned much in my tours of first Scotland and then England, Wales and Ireland. I now will look further afield; to Europe, which has a surprising number of whisky distilleries and many interesting golf courses; to North America, where whisky and golf have strong connections with both Scotland and Ireland; and to the Far East and Australasia where from India to Japan to Tasmania whisky and golf are both thriving. I think I also need to return to Scotland, particularly as there is so much activity in the whisky industry.

As a Scot I take considerable pride in this universal appeal. I have learned plenty in my travels so far and hope to learn more. While discovering what connects these two great pastimes, I also am forming views, a personal manifesto, on how they should develop. Here there are some differences. Golf needs to return more to its roots, become a little less serious and a little more instinctive. Golf would benefit from less shot ritual and more impulse. Let us hope that the new simplified rules, with the advisory time for you to take your shot within 40 seconds, will speed the game up. More players should try foursomes golf rather than endless 3 or 4 ball medal play. Courses should be more natural, more environmentally sensitive and less contrived.

Whisky on the other hand could do with a little more ritual. In an environment of lower alcohol consumption the prize for whisky lies in quality and diversity. I am in favour of spending more time deciding which whisky to choose (certainly more than 40 seconds) and then contemplating and savouring it rather than swigging it.

In summary we should look to take less time playing more golf and take more time drinking less whisky.

Andrew Brown
January 2019

Bibliography

While there are numerous fine books on both whisky and golf the following were particularly relevant to this book

Malt Whisky
 Charles MacLean   Lomond Books 2013

Whiskey A Global History
 Kevin R Kosar   Reaktion Books 2016

Maclean's Miscellany of Whisky
 Charles MacLean   Little Books Ltd. 2015

A Glass Apart Irish Single Pot Still Whiskey
 Fionnán O'Connor   Images Publishing 2017

The World Atlas of Whisky
 Dave Broom   Hachette 2014

The Whisky Distilleries of the United Kingdom
 Alfred Barnard   Birlinn Ltd. 2018

Malt Whisky Yearbook 2019   MagDig Media 2018

Sand and Golf, How terrain shapes the game
 George Waters   Goff Books 2013

The 100 Greatest Ever Golfers
 Andy Farrell   Elliott & Thompson 2011

Methods of early golf architecture
 The selected writings of Alister MacKenzie,
H.S Colt and A. W. Tillinghast,   Coventry House Publishing 2013

The Spirit of St Andrews
 Alister MacKenzie   Broadway Books